The Cognitive Enterprise

Landmark Books by Meghan-Kiffer Press

Cognitive Computing
A Brief Guide for Game Changers

Business Process Management
The Next Wave

Business Architecture
The Art and Practice of Business Transformation

Dot Cloud
The 21st Century business Platform Built on Cloud Computing

Business Innovation in the Cloud
Strategies for Executing on Innovation with Cloud Computing

Value Networks
And the True Nature of Collaboration

Smart Process Apps
The Next Breakout Business Advantage

Dot.Cloud
The 21st Century business Platform Built on Cloud Computing

Enterprise Cloud Computing
A Strategy Guide for Business and Technology Leaders

Extreme Competition
Innovation and the Great 21st Century Business Reformation

Business Process Management
The Third Wave

Mastering the Unpredictable
How Adaptive Case Management Will Revolutionize
the Way That Knowledge Workers Get Things Done

IT Doesn't Matter
Business Processes Do

The Real-Time Enterprise
Competing on Time

See more at...

Meghan-Kiffer Press

www.mkpress.com

Innovation at the Intersection of Business and Technology

The Cognitive Enterprise

"All is Changed, Changed Utterly"
—William Butler Yeates, 1916

Bob Lewis

Scott Lee

Meghan-Kiffer Press

Tampa, Florida, USA

www.mkpress.com

Innovation at the Intersection of Business and Technology

Publisher's Cataloging-in-Publication Data

Lewis, Bob and Scott Lee.
The Cognitive Enterprise / Bob Lewis, Scott Lee, - 1st ed.
p. cm.
Includes bibliographic entries and index.
  ISBN-10: 0-929652-55-X ISBN-13: 978-0-929652-55-9
  1. Management 2. Technological innovation. 3. Diffusion of innovations.
  4. Globalization—Economic aspects. 5. Information technology. 6. Information Society. 7. Organizational change. I. Lewis, Scott Lee. II. Title

HM48.L75 2015
303.48'33–dc22   CIP

Published by Meghan-Kiffer Press
310 East Fern Street — Suite G
Tampa, FL 33604 USA

Any product mentioned in this book may be a trademark of its company.

Meghan-Kiffer books are available at special quantity discounts for
corporate education and training use. For more information, write
Special Sales, Meghan-Kiffer Press, Suite G, 310 East Fern Street,
Tampa, Florida 33604, or email info@mkpress.com

Meghan-Kiffer Press

Tampa, Florida, USA

Innovation at the Intersection of Business and Technology

Printed in the United States of America.   SAN 249-7980
MK Printing 10 9 8 7 6 5 4 3 2 1

Table of Contents

FOREWORD BY THOMAS H. DAVENPORT 8

FOREWORD BY PETER FINGAR... 10

PREFACE.. 12

PROLOG 15

INTRODUCTION 18

1. A GRAB BAG OF CHANGE DRIVERS.. 25
    CANARIES 25
    STAY-THE-SAME TO CHANGE RATIO... 26
    STRATIFICATION OF WEALTH... 28
    ATTITUDES ABOUT TECHNOLOGY... 28
    TYPES OF TECHNOLOGY 29
    ATTITUDES ABOUT EMPLOYMENT... 29
    REMOTE WORKERS 30
    TEAMWORK.. 31

2. THE END OF FINANCE 35
    CANARIES IN THE COAL MINE 35
    MISSION MATTERS 38
    THE CONSEQUENCES OF FOCUSING ON FINANCES 39
    YOU'RE HIRING WHOM? 40
    CEO COMPENSATION... 42
    SOCIALISM? 43
    COST CUTTING IN THE COGNITIVE ENTERPRISE 43
    THE FINALE.. 45

3. PERMEABILITY.. 47
    CANARIES IN THE COAL MINE 47
    THE ETG.. 51
    OPEN SOURCE IS NOT SOFTWARE! 55
    TESLA: EXPLOITING PERMEABILITY.. 56
    APPLE: RESISTING PERMEABILITY 58
    PERMEABLE OR PERMEABLE BY DESIGN 59
    THE WORKSPACE IS EVERYWHERE! 60
    PUTTING IT ALL TOGETHER 61

4. THE DECLINE OF METRICS 62
    CANARIES IN THE COAL MINE 62
    COROLLARY #1: IF YOU CAN MEASURE, MOST LIKELY YOU STILL CAN'T MANAGE 67

COROLLARY #2: IF YOU MIS-MEASURE YOU'LL MISMANAGE 70
WHAT MAKES A USEFUL SYSTEM OF METRICS 75
WHAT METRICS ARE FOR 77
ANALYTICS ARE THE NEW METRICS 79

5. JUDGMENT DAY 85
CANARIES 85
JUDGMENT DAY 85
THINKING 101 86
OODA 95
WHAT A COGNITIVE ENTERPRISE KNOWS 97
METRICS PROVIDE INFORMATION. ANALYTICS PROVIDE KNOWLEDGE 98
PROFILING 99
PSYCHOGRAPHIC PROFILES 101
KINETIC PROFILES 103
CONSUMPTION PROFILE 104
IS IT REAL? 107
REAL-WORLD EXPERIENCE 111

6. THE COGNITIVE MODEL 113
CANARY 113
CUSTOMERS 113
COMMUNITIES 118
CAPABILITIES 121

7. THE END OF THE INDUSTRIAL PROCESS PANACEA 125
CANARIES IN THE COAL MINE 125
INDUSTRIAL PROCESSES VS. PRACTICE 128
PRACTICE DESIGN 133
COGNITIVE PROCESSES 138

8. INDUSTRIAL-AGE IT VS. COGNITIVE-AGE IT 147
CANARY IN THE COAL MINE 147
INFORMATION TECHNOLOGY AND THE COGNITIVE ENTERPRISE 151
INFORMATION TECHNOLOGY AND THE RISE OF BUSINESS PRACTICES 152
IT SPENDING RATIOS AND WHAT TO DO ABOUT THEM 154
THE PERVASIVE TECHNOLOGY ERA 156
SHADOW IT AND THE INTEGRATION PARTNER ORGANIZATION 159
THE BIG FINISH 163

9. LEADING A COGNITIVE ENTERPRISE 164
ACCOUNTABILITY VS. RESPONSIBILITY 168
FOLLOWERSHIP 171

THE COGNITIVE ENTERPRISE VS. THE SILOED ENTERPRISE.................................... 173
CULTURE.. 182

10: THE WAY FORWARD IS A SLIPPERY SLOPE **187**
ENTERPRISE ARCHITECTURE.. 188
PROGRESSIVE: USING TECHNOLOGY TO MAKE THE BUSINESS SMARTER 192
WHO ... OR WHAT ... WILL BE IN CHARGE? 194
MAINFRAMES VS. PERSONAL COMPUTERS 197
THE HMRI.. 199

EPILOG **202**

INDEX **204**

ABOUT THE AUTHORS **206**

ACKNOWLEDGEMENTS **208**

COMPANION BOOKS FROM MEGHAN-KIFFER PRESS **210**

Foreword by Thomas H. Davenport

"To make knowledge work productive will be the great management task of this century, just as to make manual work productive was the great management task of the last century." — Peter Drucker, Age of Discontinuity, p.290. The date for this book was 1969, and by "this century" Drucker meant the 20th. We are now well into the 21st century, of course, and Drucker's mandate is still relevant; we didn't achieve that knowledge work productivity objective in the 20th century.

Central to much thinking about how organizations should be restructured for the 21st century is the idea that innovation and growth will depend more and more on so-called knowledge workers, the sort of people who, to quote the title of my book, find themselves "Thinking for a Living." And they won't be thinking alone.

Knowledge work is a collaborative activity, and it should be an inclusive one as well. One of the secrets of Toyota's success is that the company encourages every worker, no matter how far down the production line, to consider himself a knowledge worker and to think creatively about incrementally improving his particular corner of the organization. Each worker also has many opportunities to discuss potential improvements with coworkers.

And the participation should not be restricted to knowledge workers inside your company. Numerous instances can be cited in which high-performing knowledge workers attribute much of their success to their networks. We have over three billion minds connected across the globe via mobile technologies and the Internet. Today's "knowledge management" is decidedly inter-organizational.

What about today's Millennials, for whom informal knowledge sharing is the casual norm? In The Cognitive Enterprise, Lewis and Lee write, "This isn't a generation that makes conscious, case-by-case decisions about technology. It's a genera-

8

tion accustomed to technology being pervasive, used wherever it makes their lives more comfortable or convenient. Its members expect technology to be present when and where they want it, working the way it's supposed to work. Pervasive. Don't call them Millennials. Call them the Embedded Technology Generation (ETG)."

Much of my work since the business process reengineering movement in the early 90s has involved applying technology to knowledge management and analytics. The march of both technology and business innovation are unstoppable. The complexity of business processes has grown exponentially. We need to connect the dots among business process management, knowledge management, and analytics, especially in a world in which mobile and social technologies have transformed how people communicate, work, live —and think. The authors of this book argue that the cognitive enterprise will be driven by customers, communities and capabilities. The cognitive enterprise embeds cognitive people augmented with cognitive technology to put smart decision-making into the core of the business. In this book the authors set the stage for the cognitive enterprise, and that should give any reader something to cogitate and act upon.

Thomas H. Davenport
Distinguished Professor of IT and Management, Babson College
Co-Founder and Research Director, International Institute for Analytics, Research Fellow, MIT Center for Digital Business
Senior Advisor to Deloitte Analytics, and author of *Thinking for a Living* and *Competing on Analytics*. www.tomdavenport.com

Foreword by Peter Fingar

"It's tough to make predictions, especially about the future."
— Yogi Berra

"The future is already here -- it's just not very evenly distributed."
— William Gibson

We are in the early stages of an era of *exponential* change. Digital innovations are remaking our industries, economy, and society just as steam, electricity, and internal combustion did to usher us in to an era beyond the Agricultural Age where our great and great-great grandparents toiled on farms.

Indeed, change itself has changed. As the authors write in this book, "People, process, technology. When running a business we have to think in these terms, or so we're told by those who tell us such things. We've said such things ourselves.

"But while they say 'people' first, most often these business experts actually put process in first place. Technology comes in second, playing an important supporting role.

"People, when they finally make an appearance, show up as occupiers of new roles they must be taught for the new process to be successful, adherents of a culture that must be changed for the new process to be successful, and occupants of the boxes that make up the org chart – boxes that have to be rearranged so the new process can be successful.

"The 'people' part of the formula mostly represents an irritating contributor to organizational change resistance – something that must be overcome. So, it's really PROCESS, Technology, *people*.

"While dehumanizing, this perspective worked pretty well for the industrial age of business. The industrial age was all about scale and repetition – qualities human beings are notoriously bad at, in no small part because we don't enjoy them."

But now, we are well beyond the industrial age and it's time to move on to PEOPLE, Process, *technology*. We live in a world of *exponential change*, a change driven by globalization, global connections, aging explosion of global populations, the robotization of manufacturing and technological changes in the arenas of biotech, nanotech, genomics sequencing, solar, the Internet of Everything and cognitive computing.

Customers, Collaboration and Capabilities are at the heart of the shift to PEOPLE, Process, *technology*... moving far away from *command and control, mass-production economies*, and on to *connect and collaborate, mass customization economies*. Your fancy corporate Web site is the last place consumers go to evaluate your offerings ... they connect and collaborate with social media.

What does all this mean? And what should you be doing to remain viable — starting today?

Read this book, and act on it!

Peter Fingar

Author of *Cognitive Computing: A Brief Guide for Game Changers*, and 23 more books including the seminal book, *Business Process Management: The Third Wave*. www.peterfingar.com

Preface

Before we get to any point at all, a warning: **This isn't your usual business book.**

In particular, this isn't a work of scholarship. While we occasionally do cite actual research, and do our best to give credit where it's due, this is mostly a book of ideas we've both been developing over a matter of years. They're based on our experience working at all levels of corporations of differing sizes and a wide variety of industries; also our experience consulting with corporations of widely differing sizes in an equally wide variety of industries.

It's a book that's as much about street smarts as it is about academically tested hypotheses.

What it isn't is the book we started to write.

When we first started this project, we thought we were going to be writing about the societal enterprise.

Every enterprise is, after all, a society, and much of what you're about to read is just as pertinent when thinking of the enterprise in those terms as when you're thinking of it as a potentially cognitive entity.

As we wrote, we discovered that while all the subjects we were writing about matter a great deal when thinking about what it takes for a modern business to succeed, not all of them were especially relevant to the societal view of the enterprise.

Quite the opposite.

The more we thought about the nature of societies and the more we thought about how large enterprises undeniably are societies, it reinforced our view that business executives have to be very conscious of how their leadership affects the nature of the societies they lead.

It's just that our initial premise – that executives who make this the centerpiece of their responsibilities will find that this is the secret to competitive success – never seemed to take hold in our own thoughts.

It was more what logicians would call a contrapositive: Executives who ignore the societal nature of the organizations they lead will find themselves at the top of a failing, slowly failing but still failing, business.

A book about what you have to do to avoid failure struck us as insufficiently ambitious and weakly useful at best.

Meanwhile, in our consulting we were reminded every time we talked with a client about the biggest challenges most executives face. And to our eyes there is one huge difference between businesses that work and businesses that don't: *businesses that work have a lot in common with predators, while those that don't work have more in common with habitats.*

Predators have a clear purpose and are very good at achieving it. Habitats have no sense of purpose. They are places critters that do have a sense of purpose use to accomplish it.

We thought back to Microsoft in its early, explosively successful days. Its defining characteristic was predation. Like many predators, it observed the herd (other technology companies), identified the herd's weakest members, and took them down: CPM, Lotus, WordPerfect, IBM's OS/2 division, and Novell.

We thought about discussions we've had with a range of senior executives and as we did, the point seemed to spring into sharp focus.

Executives who chose a competitor to beat, chose it wisely, and knew when to shift to a new, better competitor to beat were the ones that seemed to lead organizations that not only won in the marketplace, but were effective internally as well.

Those who developed strategies that ignored the whole notion that competitors matter, on the other hand, seemed to always preside over habitats instead, with executives and managers who built high silo walls and expended most of their competitive energies beating the department down the hall.

We looked at what we'd already written and discovered we'd been writing about what it takes for a business to act with coherent purpose all along.

We'd just been fighting it.

So we stopped fighting it and started thinking about the next level beyond acting with purpose. That seemed clear once we were pointed in the right direction. Companies that act with purpose already seem to have a strong advantage over their habitat-oriented brethren. Companies that are smart about it seem to have an insurmountable advantage.

As business consultants we know: For our clients, an insurmountable advantage is a very good thing to have.

As authors, our purpose is to help your business achieve one.

—Bob Lewis   *—Scott Lee*

Dedication

This book is dedicated to CIOs and IT leaders around the world. All of them. When something goes wrong in the business, it's the CIO who's usually left holding the bag. Even when they do something exceptionally well (the Y2K crisis was an example) instead of receiving appreciation, they find out nobody believed there was anything important to be done.

So to all of you CIOs and IT leaders: You're blamed when things go wrong and you're blamed when things go right. We want you to know that we, at least, appreciate your efforts.

Prolog

They're the sixth consecutive Worst Generation Yet.

They're self-absorbed, have no work ethic, are entitled, and their cell phones are glued to their hands. They're…

No, they're not. Forget all that nonsense.

We're talking about the generation commonly called "Millennials," and generalizations about them are about as valid as any generalization about any group is. Which is to say, you can always find enough examples to satisfy your confirmation bias if you're so inclined.

Beyond that, this generation really does have two characteristics that truly and uniquely belong to it. Because of these characteristics they'll change the world.

For the first, go back to the Greatest Generation. After World War II, its members expected to be able to work for the same employer until the day they retired. Most did.

But in the 1970s a very different social contract replaced the mutual employee/employer loyalty that was a hallmark of the 1950s and '60s, one that persists to this day – the at-will employer/employee relationship.

This isn't what's new to Millennials. It started in their grandparents' day. What's new: This is the first generation to grow up in a world where cradle-to-grave employment never existed. As a result, unlike their forebears they have no expectation of employer loyalty.

We'll explore the ramifications of this in Chapters 3 and 5. They are profound.

Even more profound:

Those of us who worked the help desk in the 1980s and 1990s remember the jokes and sneering stories – users who corrected typos by putting WiteOut® on their computer screen, whose modems didn't work because they were actually answering machines, and who, for the most part, couldn't find their posteriors with both hands and a map, descending into a terrified palsy whenever they had to learn something new or different that involved their keyboard and mouse.

Faced with this widespread technophobia, IT was forced into a bizarre defensive mode, catering to users' perceived limitations by, for example, when installing a new, more capable system, doing everything possible to make it behave just like the old, less-capable one.

But Millennials' infant toys were driven by microprocessors. They adapted to new user interfaces before they learned to walk; now they try out new social media sites and massive multiplayer online games by poking around to see what happens. They've never heard of WiteOut®, and when they contact the help desk the problem is just as likely to be the result of an IT mess-up as something they did wrong.

And if it was the result of something they did wrong, it was likely a highly sophisticated sort of mistake.

This isn't a generation that makes conscious, case-by-case decisions about technology either. This is a generation that shares experiences in real time through photos taken with cell phones and posted to Snapchat or Facebook, because that's how you share experiences with your friends, of course.

It's a generation accustomed to technology being pervasive, used wherever it makes their lives more comfortable or convenient. Its members expect technology to be present when and where they want it, working the way it's supposed to work.

Pervasive.

Don't call them Millennials. Call them the **Embedded Technology Generation (ETG)** because along with their low expectations of employer loyalty, it's how thoroughly technology is embedded in their lives that's their defining characteristic.

Is membership in the ETG purely generational? Of course not. Grandparents routinely Skype their grandkids while making friends they never meet all over the world on Facebook, just as they had pen pals when they were young and penmanship mattered. Most of us have joined it to at least a limited extent.

But for the most part, the older the user, the more left-brain our use of technology is. For the ETG, technology is intuitive, and if it isn't, someone had better hire better designers; Google is the new memory; and the Encyclopedia Britannica is something they might read about, by accident, in Wikipedia.

For the ETG, whose members each carry more computing power in their hands than existed during the struggle to crack Enigma, technology is an expected and pervasive part of their lives ... integrated into it, not a separate category of stuff.

If a business they work in isn't just like this – if its systems aren't seamless and natural – it means the business isn't organized very well.

In a very real sense, the ETG is the first generation of cyborgs. Its members are our first experiment in computer-augmented humanity. And if you find that thought horrifying, the alternative is far, far worse and more dehumanizing – a topic we'll take up in the final chapter of this book.

For now:

This isn't a book *about* the ETG. But it is a book that probably wouldn't have been necessary if it weren't for the ETG. It's the harbinger of many of the changes that have led to the need for the cognitive enterprise.

Introduction

People, process, technology.

When running a business we have to think in these terms, or so we're told by those who tell us such things. We've said such things ourselves.

But while they say "people" first, most often these business experts actually put process in first place. Technology comes in second, playing an important supporting role.

People, when they finally make an appearance, show up as occupiers of new roles they must be taught for the new process to be successful, adherents of a culture that must be changed for the new process to be successful, and occupants of the boxes that make up the org chart – boxes that have to be rearranged so the new process can be successful.

The "people" part of the formula, that is, mostly represents an irritating contributor to organizational change resistance – something that must be overcome.

It's really PROCESS, Technology, *people*.

While dehumanizing, this perspective worked pretty well for the industrial age of business. The industrial age was all about scale and repetition – qualities human beings are notoriously bad at, in no small part because we don't enjoy them.

Organizations "designed by geniuses to be run by idiots" was pretty much the game plan for the industrial age. Instead of operating through practices that were as smart as the smartest practitioner, businesses operated according to processes designed with a focus on simplification and standardization. These aren't bad things in themselves, but they're unfortunate in how they encourage employees to turn off their brains when they enter the building.

Businesses built to this model – call it the "industrial model" – are anything but cognitive. They're nothing like an entity that pays attention to the world around it, evaluates itself and its changing situation, and continually adapts. This is true even in companies whose managers sincerely embrace concepts like continuous improvement. There's a difference, after all, between improving a process and bypassing it entirely to improvise when the process just doesn't fit a particular situation.

This industrial mindset is so pervasive that even companies that aren't in the business of creating lots of identical copies of things, have, to their detriment, adopted practices of the industrial model because that's "best practice" – a phrase that should be taken out and shot.

The industrial PROCESS, Technology, *people* model rests on a set of hidden assumptions, that, like most hidden assumptions, were reasonable when they were first made. The problem with hidden assumptions, though, is that when the world changes and they're no longer valid, they're still hidden and so remain unchallenged.

For more and more businesses, the industrial perspective and the hidden assumptions it rests on are obsolete. A constellation of forces are making them an impediment to success.

For this growing population of businesses to thrive, they, and very likely, "they" includes your business, will need to change their thinking.

Before we get to that, there's one hidden assumption that has to go by the wayside immediately. It's the assumption that businesses are just like people, only bigger. Yes, they've been found to be, for many legal purposes, persons. But they aren't. Nor are they merely the sum of the individual human beings who work in and for them, any more than you are merely the sum of your intestines, spleen, brain, and so on.

As life forms, human beings are more than their component parts. Businesses are, too. They're an artificial life form, created by human beings but non-human in their anatomy, physiology, and behavior. Among the differences, two stand out:

Humans are presumptively moral. Businesses are demonstrably amoral. We rightly assume most of the people around us, most of the time, aren't going to behave in ways that are excessively nasty. The laws we pass are (or should be) based on our consensus sense of what's right and wrong, and the systems set up to enforce them are scaled to the assumption that people who violate them are the exception.

Businesses, in contrast, have as the bedrock principle of their

19

moral code their fiduciary responsibility to their shareholders. In some cases, business executives are overt about their decision-making in this regard: If the fine for breaking a law or regulation is smaller than the profit to be made by doing so, then the violation is good business and the fine is the cost of doing it.

The amorality of business is not a topic we'll be covering in this book. We mention it here only to help demonstrate that corporations are fundamentally different from people, including the people who lead and work in them.

Human beings think before making decisions. Businesses, in contrast, aren't intrinsically cognitive entities. To be fair about it, many human beings don't think very hard before making many of their decisions. But they do have the capacity. It's innate, and depending on one's background, encouraged.

The closest equivalents to human-style thinking businesses have are the governance mechanisms that in principle make some business decision-making independent of the foibles of the individual human beings involved.

But governance is often window-dressing, with actual decision-making the result of horse-trading among the human beings who are supposed to be acting in the corporation's best interests. It's also commonly slow and cumbersome, unsurprising given that the fundamental building block of most governance is the committee.

For the rest, businesses make decisions, but not by thinking. If this strikes you as impossible, consider that amoebas make decisions without the benefit of a central nervous system, let alone a brain.

Don't misunderstand. The men and women who make decisions on behalf of the business are often individually quite intelligent. The business they work for gets the benefit of their individual intelligence, along with the more dubious benefit of committee-based intelligence, as the myriad decisions needed for a business to survive from day to day get made, one way or another.

But the business isn't making them. In most cases the knowledge, experience, and judgment that goes into them is in no way institutionalized.

But enough of that. This isn't going to be an abstract treatise on applying theories of cognition to corporate governance. Ugh.

Our goal isn't to bore you to death. It's to provide practical guidance on making an organization behave more like an intelligent, purposeful organism and less like a directionless ecosystem.

The what and why of the cognitive enterprise

What we mean by "cognitive enterprise" is one that behaves as if it had its own intelligence and purpose.

Consider the difference between an organism and an ecosystem and it will be clear. Organisms act as a whole. As entities they make decisions, whether they're as simple as an amoeba or as complex as *Homo sapiens*.

Ecosystems are just as complex as organisms, more complex once you include the complexity of the organisms that comprise them, but don't act with purpose. While ecosystems have emergent properties beyond those of their component organisms, any "decision" an ecosystem makes is the accidental direction set through the "invisible hand" of all the plants and critters that live in it.

Most large enterprises are more like ecosystems than organisms, hence the old phrase, "It's a jungle out there."

Our definition of a cognitive enterprise is one that acts more like an organism, one where business decisions are about the success of the business in its environment.

The point and purpose of this book is to make business decisions of all kinds and at all levels smarter, to make the business, if not truly cognitive in the sense of being an entity capable of human-style thinking, at least an entity that mimics it in rudimentary but useful ways.

It will be quite a journey.

The modern theory of the business is that it's an independent entity. Its employees at all levels, from the board of directors and top executives through every individual contributor, are supposed to act as agents of the business, subordinating their personal preferences by inferring what the wishes and preferences of the business would be, if it was in fact capable of the sort of cognition that would give it wishes and preferences. As businesses aren't just people only bigger, asking people to do this is intrinsically dehumanizing.

Which wouldn't matter a bit if it was good business. But as it turns out, it isn't. Quite the opposite. If we humans do no more than act as agents of the business, an inhuman entity that isn't capable of thinking, the result is dumbing down the workforce so its members aren't allowed to apply their intelligence and judgment to the business decisions they make on the business's behalf.

This book's goal is to change all that, to make businesses, not just the people who run them, but the businesses themselves, smarter. As a fringe benefit, we expect businesses that follow this path to be less de-humanizing as well.

Cognitive is the word we're going to use throughout this book, in the sense that the entities that are businesses will have to do a closer approximation to thinking than they needed to during the industrial age of business.

Done well, they'll "think" in ways that are closer to how human beings think about things.

That's what this book is about: How the hidden assumptions that led to the wholesale de-humanization of business are less and less valid, what the new circumstances are that are supplanting them, and what to do about it all.

The plan ...

We've divided this book into two sections: Driving Forces, and What to Do About Them and What Not to Do.

The Driving Forces section includes four chapters, not counting the prolog. The emergence of the Embedded Technology Generation is a long-term and profound driving force. Even those of us who aren't members of the ETG have been profoundly influenced by its culture and norms (curmudgeons would say "contaminated.") The pervasiveness of, and comfort with, increasingly advanced technology is an important driver, and key enabler of the cognitive enterprises to come.

The prolog is about the world-changing impact of people who, far from being intimidated by new technologies, are so in tune with them that learning the next one is about as challenging a task as figuring out the controls for a rental car is for an average business traveler before driving it off the lot.

Chapter 1 isn't about a single driver. It's a grab bag of forces that are crucial for understanding the need to run a more cognitive enterprise, but these forces just aren't complex enough to warrant full chapters. They're fundamental enough, though, that nothing else in the book will make much sense without taking them into account.

Chapter 2 takes aim at the notion that focusing on the financials is the proper province of business executives. It isn't. This chapter explains what the proper province is, and why.

You might find Chapter 3 even more disconcerting. Its premise: Unlike industrial age businesses, cognitive enterprises are intrinsically *permeable,* and rather than try to fight this challenge, businesses will be better-served to see permeability as an immense competitive advantage for those whose heads are screwed on the right way.

Chapter 4 takes aim at the current obsession with metrics, a critical component of any well-run industrial enterprise. Our reliance on metrics is, you'll find, excessive and misplaced in a cognitive enterprise, because it's one of the most telling symptoms of the non-cognitive nature of business and business decision-making. What makes this a driving force behind the emerging cognitive enterprise is the rise of analytics as an alternative to traditional metrics. What's the connection? Read the chapter and find out.

Chapter 5's role is pivotal. It takes the old data/ information/ knowledge/wisdom pyramid, inserts a key missing layer (judgment), puts the whole thing on a more solid footing, and connects it to the previous chapter's points about metrics and analytics. In a book about the cognitive enterprise it's where we put thinking in context.

The PROCESS, Technology, *people* model was designed for the industrial age. Chapter 6 introduces its replacement – customers, communities and capabilities – and explains how this new model works.

If PROCESS, Technology, *people* has to be replaced with a new model, does this mean business processes themselves have become irrelevant to business success? No, not exactly, although the confining nature and ambiguous definition of "process" has become an impediment. Chapter 7 provides a more expansive view of how businesses can and should get things done.

Strange but true: The occasional business pundit notwithstanding, Information Technology matters. Beyond this, much of what's driving the need for businesses to become more cognitive are the threats and opportunities to current business models and strategies driven by new capabilities provided and shaped by information technology. Chapter 8 looks at how information technology organizations will have to change to stay relevant in a cognitive enterprise.

And finally, in Chapter 9, it will be time to look at leadership and what that will look like in cognitive businesses. When it comes to the transformation itself, leadership will be the starting point. We hold leadership to Chapter 9 because without a full understanding of the nature of the change, our discussion of leadership would be context-free.

None of the driving forces we identify and none of the responses to them we suggest are once-and-done events. Chapter 10 takes an uncertain look into the future of the cognitive enterprise, and in particular some potential ways information technology might evolve that could change the nature of cognition itself.

While Chapter 10 might, from here, sound like a tiresome exercise in second-rate science fiction, in fact it will point out situations that even now are becoming factors business leaders in some industries are starting to have to deal with.

That's the plan. Writing this book turned out to be more complicated and challenging than we ever imagined when we started the effort.

If we've done our job, you won't find reading it to be anywhere near as complicated and challenging.

1. A Grab Bag of Change Drivers

Canaries

Whether or not you've ever held pick and shovel to dig coal out of the ground, you undoubtedly know what canaries were used for in coal mines before the advent of modern air-quality-monitoring technology. They monitored air quality the old fashioned way by losing consciousness or dying when it was bad, long before it became bad enough for the human beings around them to notice.

In this book, our canaries are metaphorical. We'd never stoop to using a helpless bird to keep us from suffocating. These are anecdotes about modern business situations. Their role is to illustrate what each chapter is about. Not to serve as proof – as someone once said, the plural of anecdote is not data – but to illustrate.

Unlike coal-mine canaries, some of ours will describe situations in which a business thrived. But like coal-mine canaries, others will describe business collapses, hardships, or other situations where failing to recognize the societal nature of a business and deal with it accordingly did serious damage.

Canary

In 1968, IBM introduced a database management system called IMS. For a number of technical reasons, it's widely understood to be hopelessly obsolete.

IBM estimates 95% of the Fortune 1,000 continue to rely on it as an important component of their technical architecture. That reliance means a huge loss of flexibility, as databases stored in IMS are harder to manage and reconfigure than databases stored in more modern technologies. It also means dependence on information technology professionals willing to take jobs that paint their careers into metaphorical corners, because while IMS continues to be essential, it isn't where the good jobs are in IT. Even for the companies that rely on it, it's something they want to in-

25

vest in as little as possible because of its intrinsic limitations.

Which means the companies that still use IMS have two choices: 1) employing older programmers and database administrators (DBAs) who are close enough to retirement that staying with something familiar and comfortable is just fine; or, 2) employing younger programmers and DBAs who don't have enough skill to get one of the good jobs in IT.

Why don't these companies replace IMS? It's usually because conversions are expensive and time consuming. Whatever its limitations, IMS still works, and there's always a more urgent project that needs the budget and staff.

The reasons to replace IMS are strategic, architectural, and competitive – they have logic on their side, but not strong, provable financial returns on investment.

Often, nobody really knows what's there, except for one or two grizzled veterans who have that knowledge in their heads and have no particular reason to write it all down: A conversion effort wouldn't just be expensive and time-consuming, it would be risky as well.

And so, in important ways, these corporate behemoths are trying to win races with competitors that are driving Lamborghinis, while they're sitting atop a hippopotamus.

That the world of business is changing is a boring truism. Everyone knows it. Everyone knows the pace of change is accelerating.

But what exactly is it that's changing? That depends on your perspective. Here's ours:

Stay-the-Same to Change Ratio

Yes, the pace of change is accelerating. Acceleration of the pace of change has been the one constant in business thinking since we first started thinking seriously about business, and probably long before then. Not a new insight.

What gets less attention than the accelerating pace of change itself is that this isn't what causes such a stir. The stir comes from how it shrinks the useful lifetime of business investments.

It's the ratio of how long investments last; how long things stay the same; and to when they approach the end of their useful life i.e., the outcome of change.

Not just investments in infrastructure, either. Investments in products, assembly lines, business processes and supplier relationships. No matter what your business does, the specifics will last for less time next year than they did last year.

But even that isn't the problem. The problem is, in most businesses what's needed to set your business up to deliver these things takes just as much time as it always did, or nearly so.

Oversimplifying just a bit (but not by much), having your business do what it does, day in and day out, is called operations. Changing your business to do something different tomorrow than it did yesterday is what projects are for. Designing a new product and bringing it to market takes a project. Manufacturing and distributing it every day is operations.

Operations are equal to "staying the same," and efficient operations depend on infrastructure. Infrastructure is expensive and it is time-consuming to get it right. Because of this it has to last a long time. The challenging consequence is that infrastructure out lasts strategy, let alone products and services, and certainly the marketing campaigns that sell your products and services.

The more infrastructure your business has, the more constraints this places on your future strategic choices.

Projects = making things different, things including such matters as your business infrastructure.

So when the stay-the-same/change ratio shrinks, it means that, relatively speaking, project management increases in importance relative to operations management. And one interesting property of projects is that more of them fail or deliver unsatisfactory results than are successful.

And yet, it's commonplace for businesses to treat project management as a sort of bridge position – a place to try out promising employees to see if they might have what it takes to succeed in *real* management, also known as managing an operating department.

Project management is not as commonplace as it used to be. There are enlightened businesses that recognize the importance of project management as its own career track, just not as many as there should be.

Stratification of wealth

The middle class is shrinking while an ever-increasing share of wealth is concentrated in a smaller number of households.

Why this matters here is that it inevitably drives an increased demand for luxury.

The nature of luxury is that it's comparative, not absolute. That is, if you live in a community where most people drive Fords, a Lexus is a luxury car. But if you live in a wealthy gated community, a Lexus is just a car. Luxury means you drive a Bentley, or a Maybach, or something else that costs more than a starter home for most of the population.

In the context of wealth stratification, a shift in spending patterns, from perfectly serviceable mass-produced goods to things not everyone can have, is pretty much inevitable.

Which in many ways is desirable for businesses, because one consequence of mass production is that it serves competitive markets, commoditizing goods and driving down margins – a situation widely understood by business executives everywhere to be a Bad Thing.

While the demand for mass produced goods certainly won't go away, the growing marketplace will be for luxury, things not everyone can have, and ideally things nobody else can have.

So where standardization and simplification are beloved of process consultants everywhere, the marketplace for unique, customized, tailored goods, accompanied by high-touch personalized service is where more and more of the most profitable action will be.

Attitudes about technology

Technology used to be intimidating. Then it became the new normal. Now it's embedded in peoples' lifestyles. For many, and in particular among those now entering the workforce and ranks of high-value consumers (the ETG) it's part of the background. But even among older age cohorts, technology is far more familiar and accepted than it was even ten years ago.

28

Types of technology

Employees as assets?

"Our employees are our greatest asset." It's a cliché. And it's absurd. Assets appear on the balance sheet; employees only appear on the income-and-expense statement.

The problem: As the chapter on metrics will point out in more depth, you get what you measure, and only what you measure. As employee asset-hood isn't measured in the company's financial systems, employees aren't really considered assets.

Whether they should appear as an asset is a very different matter. It's telling that when Steve Jobs passed away, Apple's balance sheet was unaffected, even though he truly was the company's single most important asset.

At its peak, global landline penetration rates never exceeded 25 percent of the world's population, but as of this writing there are more mobile devices than people on this earth.[1] Space-age gadgets that were staples of science fiction in movies and cartoons 25 years ago are now in the pockets of teenagers, who very likely have more technical computing power than you provide your employees. As your organization tries to manage change, the outside world is adopting new and better ways to communicate through social networks, measure their health with wearable tech, and manage their world through connected things.

Attitudes about employment

It's been a long time since employers truly considered employees to be an asset. Expensive aggravation is a better description of how many employers view their employees were they to be honest about their attitudes. "Fungible commodity" is how many more think about the subject.

The workforce is catching up, or perhaps catching on. While precise and reliable data are hard to come by, the survey data that are available, collected by the Freelancers Union, suggest that, at

---

[1] Source: Cisco Visual Networking Index: Global Mobile Data Traffic Forecast Update, 2013–2018

least in the U.S., about one third of the workforce is, in some way, shape or form, independent. Moreover, the age weighting is significant. Younger members of the workforce are more likely to prefer this arrangement rather than relying on traditional employment.

Fewer and fewer employees are loyal to their employers because why would they be? Post-World-War II, mutual loyalty between employer and employees was both expected and real. Terminating an ineffective employee was traumatic for the manager who had to do it. Laying off employees because business was bad was the last thing business leaders did before turning off the lights for the last time.

The point here isn't that business management has become harsher, less moral, less loyal, or worse according to any moral yardstick. It's that expecting loyalty from employees in the current business climate is, depending on the person expecting it, either posturing or nonsensical.

Employees understand they're "employed at will," working under an implied contract that gives most of the power to the employer. Of course they're increasingly comfortable being independent contractors – especially so as individual health insurance is becoming, if not economical, at least more affordable compared to the cost of employer-provided group policies.

Remote workers

It's almost quaint how controversial allowing employees to work from home used to be. Now, when Yahoo!'s Marissa Mayer curtailed working from home, that's what was controversial.

Once upon a time, working from home was for employees who had well-defined tasks to work on – employees for whom "productivity" was a meaningful way to talk about their success or failure in their responsibilities.

Now? In many companies, everyone works from home unless they have a specific reason to come into the office. They're saved an annoying commute, the company saves on office space, and there's less time "wasted" in non-work-related social interactions among employees.

Remote employees are supported by collaboration technologies designed to mimic the experience of face-to-face interaction. From content management software to web conferencing to Skype, not to mention hoary old standbys like teleconferencing, email and instant messaging, collaboration without having to be in the same room is increasingly natural.

And with technical prowess, your intellectual property and tacit knowledge are more at risk than ever as employees use tools to circumvent your outdated modes of communication and infrastructure.

No, that isn't a fair assessment. What's at risk is the pretense most companies insist on that this intellectual property is in any way interesting, let alone worth defending. Your employees know better. They know that by sharing ideas they build better ideas, the value of which hugely outstrips whatever might be lost by failing to defend that which is generally so obvious that its defense is little more than full employment for lawyers.

Teamwork

According to theory, businesses are assemblages of *processes*. It's a useful theory, and if you define "process" to mean "how work gets done" – how companies turn inputs into outputs – it's even reasonable. Businesses are assemblages of processes, because what they do is to turn raw materials plus work into products and services they can sell at a profit.

There are, however, a few problems with this theory ... but we're getting ahead of ourselves.

The problem with describing enterprises as assemblages of processes is that while accurate, it isn't useful until after we take into account something more fundamental: Businesses are, first and foremost, assemblages of *relationships*. Multi-layered assemblages. In a word, communities. To understand the point, let's talk about the nature of teamwork and the mathematics of Congress.

In 1965, B.S. Tuckman published a two-factor framework accounting for team performance: trust and alignment.

Trust means exactly what you'd expect it to mean. Alignment means all team members have a shared understanding and sense of purpose. To have a high-performance team you need strong trust and close alignment.

Combine this with a bit of math and it's easy to understand why the U.S. House of Representatives doesn't stand a chance.

The House has 435 members. This means it consists of 94,395 relationships, the number of pairs of members. The formula is $n*(n-1)/2$ where n is the number of members in a group.

The U.S. House of Representatives is pretty much doomed to team dysfunction before any member even thinks about joining a political party, because really, what are the odds trust will characterize enough of these relationships to matter, even before we try for alignment to a shared, common purpose?

And it's even worse, because one problem with distrust is that it's contagious. If two members of any group don't trust each other, they don't leave it at that. They ask everyone else to choose sides – something you undoubtedly know from personal experience.

The purpose of this book, though, isn't to dissect and fix the U.S. House of Representatives, for so many reasons. It's to help business leaders make their organizations more effective.

Businesses try to dodge this relationship math by way of the organizational chart – a terribly misunderstood instrument and increasingly so as organizations try to become more cognitive.

The official purpose of the org chart is to partition responsibilities. With an org chart everyone is supposed to know their role. For many employees it's even more useful – it also explains to every executive, manager and employee what their job isn't.

Org charts are boxes within boxes, and anything outside your box is Someone Else's Problem. But the org chart is even more than that. It also defines who has to trust whom, and to what extent. Everyone inside your box is, or at least is expected to be, a member of your team. If you and I are in the same low-level box, reporting to the same supervisor, we'd better both adhere to Tuckman's definition of team members, trusting each other while sharing a common purpose. Because if we don't our supervisor will have to do something about it.

If we have different supervisors who report to the same manager we don't have to trust each other so much, and the farther apart we are on the org chart, the less important trust and alignment are to us personally.

In fact, there seems to be a law of human nature that establishes "us-ness" and "them-ness" in business by measuring the distance between us on the org chart.

The org chart serves one more purpose. In a rough, ready, inexact way it describes the enterprise's pecking order – the company's power structure and relationships.

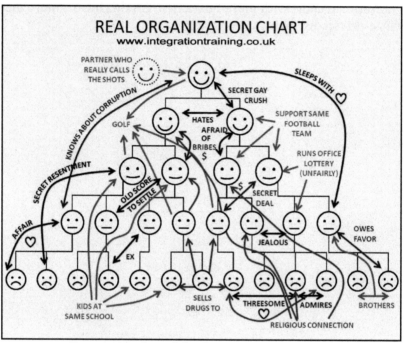

Source. Mark Walsh of Integration Training

We'll have more on org charts in the chapter on leadership. For now, recall our goal of making the enterprise more cognitive. Apply to this goal the distrust that's a natural consequence of having a traditional org chart.

Team take-homes

One key fact about alignment is that without it, trust breaks down.

One key fact about trust is that without it, everything breaks down. Business processes and practices simply don't work if Person B in the process, upon receiving the results of Person A's efforts, thinks Person A can't be trusted because with distrust comes the expectation of fault and defects. Person B won't just do his/her job. Person B will nitpick Person A's work to death, either rejecting it or angrily re-doing it.

One additional point, enterprises are increasing in size. More size means more employees. More employees mean a deeper organizational chart with more boxes in it. All this means more distance-driven distrust.

2. The End of Finance

"If we can't learn from our mistakes, what's the point in making them?" "Cy the Cynic," from Frank Stewart's bridge column

Canaries in the coal mine

Canary #1

In 2008, General Motors went off the rails.

Only that sounds like it was on the rails until 2008. It wasn't. General Motors was a train wreck that happened at three miles an hour over a span of decades. Everyone could see it coming.

Everyone, that is, except all of the executives who ran the company. They thought like economists, not competitors.

It happened like this ...

When William Durant founded General Motors in 1908, the company built cars people wanted to buy – wanted to buy them enough that they'd pay more than it cost General Motors to build them.

The difference is called profit, and General Motors made quite a bit of it.

Until 1919, when the folks running General Motors figured out they could make even more profit by financing its cars as well as manufacturing them, which worked out well for everyone.

Except for one minor problem: As years turned into decades and company management became what business schools encourage their graduates to think is sophisticated, the company's executives discovered financing was generating more profits than manufacturing.

And so General Motors cars gradually stopped being products people wanted to buy and became products General Motors had to bribe them to buy. The bribes were called rebates. They were carefully calibrated to make up the difference between the perceived value of a General Motors product and the perceived value of its foreign competitors' products while still being profitable once GMAC financing contracts were taken into account.

And so General Motors limped along, its executives doing exactly what they thought they were supposed to be doing, namely, maximizing profits and shareholder value on a quarter-by-quarter basis.

Until the bottom fell out.

Make no mistake, even without the onset of the Great Recession, General Motors was a hot mess. The reason was simple: It forgot that while its profits might have depended more on financing than on the margin from car sales, once it stopped selling cars people wanted to buy, eventually there would be nothing to finance.

Coda: In exchange for financial support from the federal government, General Motors was required to file a turnaround plan.

The first version did not include any mention of designing and building desirable products, and was rejected by the Obama administration. The second version did, and was accepted.

How sad is it that a former community organizer understood the importance of selling products people want to buy more than the highly paid executives of one of the United States' largest corporations?

Canary #2

According to *Bloomberg's* Lu Wang and Callie Bost, in the aggregate the companies that make up the S&P 500 are going to spend 95% of their earnings on dividends and stock buy-backs.

By itself this statistic is less dire, or at a minimum more ambiguous than most analysts make it out to be.

Areas companies "should" spend their money on ("should" being as much a moral as business proposition) such as labor, R&D and preventive maintenance, are pre-tax expenses. Dividends and buy-backs, in contrast, are after-tax expenses and aren't deductible.

Which means it isn't really proper to think of these as competing for the same funds. If a company were to reinvest more in its future (pre-tax) that would affect how much money is left in this-year profits to use for buybacks and dividends, but wouldn't affect what percent of profits get used this way.

It would just make the amount that percentage translates to smaller.

Move along folks. There's no story here. Or there wouldn't be were it not for two factors: (1) Executives make spending decisions with an eye to how much will be left to fund buy-backs and dividends; and (2) this year, companies aren't just returning profits to their shareholders. As reported in *Bloomberg*, "Cash returned to shareholders exceeded profits in the first quarter for the first time since 2009."

In short: Investments in what analysts delicately describe as "financial engineering" are up, and investments in the future are down.

The verdict: If this is the best use for cash the folks running the S&P 500 can come up with, it means they can't figure out how to use the money to grow their businesses.

Which is, when you come right down to it, pathetic.

There's little question, the buy-back-and-dividends vs. investing-in-the-future decision making is pure, lazy opportunism. Buy-backs in particular are a cheap trick to prop up the price of a share of stock and nothing more. Directing cash in this direction when such niggling details as preventive maintenance are underfunded is ridiculously short-sighted, akin to making sure your wine cellar is well-stocked when your car needs its oil changed.

Why might a company suffer from a paucity of investment possibilities? It seems likely the company culture discourages employees at all levels from looking for and suggesting possibilities for improvement.

And culture flows from the top, which leads to this chain of logic:

- Financial engineering is what CEOs do when they have no ideas on how to grow their businesses.
- If CEOs have no ideas, they either don't get suggestions from employees or aren't interested in them.
- If they don't get suggestions from employees, it means the company culture discourages employees from developing creative possibilities, the company culture being a product of company leadership.

And yet, boards of directors pay these CEOs enormous compensation packages for not only *not* having any ideas on how to grow the business, but actively *discouraging* everyone else from having any ideas on the subject either.

Mission matters

Every business has a mission, or should!

No, not a mission statement. Lots of businesses have those too, but they are, for the most part, information-free platitudes on which whole seconds of effort have been lavished in pursuit of substance and weeks expended on wordsmithery.

Forget mission statements. They're worthless. Unlike the company's mission, which is essential; just as essential is making sure everyone understands it – something that takes far more than a mission statement posted in large type on convenient walls.

An organization's mission is, simply stated, the social purpose the company exists to fulfill. For the cognitive enterprise, paying attention to and focusing on fulfilling the mission is a top priority – something that's equally accurate for the biggest for-profit enterprise and the smallest 401(c)3.

Although, to be accurate, large enterprises will often have more than one mission – one for each line of business. And that's okay, because as a first-order generalization, each line of business might as well be an independent business that happens to be owned by a larger business.

For the canary that opened this chapter, General Motors' mission was and is (or at least should be) to build cars people want to buy. GMAC's mission was to make cars affordable for customers who otherwise would have had to do without. Both are worthwhile missions that serve an important social purpose.

If you have no idea what your company's social purpose is and suspect there isn't one, there's a pretty good chance you're working for a company that isn't going to be around very long.

Every company also has, in addition to its mission, a business model. The business model describes the buttons and levers company decision-makers can push and pull to turn its efforts into profitable revenue.

For simple and straightforward companies the mission and business model are pretty much the same, except that the business model takes profit into account. It's the old build a better mousetrap approach to business strategy, and old as it is, it's far from the worst model for modern companies to pursue.

But not all companies are simple and straightforward, and given modern marketplaces not all companies can be simple and straightforward.

Take, for example, media companies – newspapers, magazines, and non-premium television stations in particular.

If you run a daily newspaper, for example, you might be forgiven for thinking the newspaper is your product.

One reason you might be forgiven is that from a mission perspective you'd be right. A daily newspaper's mission is to be a trusted provider of important information. The newspaper (and website) is the company's vehicle for fulfilling its mission.

That's all well and good, but newspapers have to make a profit, too. That's where the business model comes in, and from the perspective of their business model the newspaper isn't the product. For newspapers, profit comes from selling readers to advertisers. Readers are the product. The newspaper? It's bait. And this is equally true for all non-premium television stations and most magazines.

Oh, and by the way, it's worth noting that for premium cable stations like HBO, the mission and business model are the same. It's no coincidence that HBO's program quality is widely regarded as superior to most of the programming available on broadcast channels. Vastly superior. It isn't a coincidence because at HBO the business model doesn't distract anyone from its mission.

The consequences of focusing on finances

Imagine four companies that are head-to-head competitors. Company A's strategy is to sell extraordinary products. Company B's is to take incredible care of its customers. Company C's executives focus on maximizing profits, while the fine folks running Company D do everything they can to maximize shareholder value.

Your job is to predict which company will be the most profitable a few years later. It is, of course, a trick question, and so, some hints:

Company C will, predictably, cut costs. After all, the same revenue minus lower costs equals more profits.

Company D will, just as predictably, engage in financial engineering, cutting costs but also buying back stock, shifting uncuttable expenses into the next fiscal year and otherwise taking steps to impress Wall Street's easily impressed analysts.

This was a trick question because there's no way to predict whether Company A will outperform Company B or vice versa.

But it's easy to predict which of the four companies will lose market share and wallet share, because we've all watched this happen, over and over again. This is very real: Companies that cut costs and spend more time, money and energy on financial engineering than product engineering enjoy bumps in their share price, but it's like getting all your nutrition from sugar – a year or three later they crash.[2]

They have to, because company executives, like everyone else, don't have an infinite time budget to work with. Every minute they spend on financial engineering is a minute they aren't spending figuring out how to sell more products to more customers.

And, because they're engaging in financial engineering, they're taking away the wherewithal to acquire and retain customers and sell more engaging products from those closer to the action who want to make this happen.

This is true even in those companies that, as part of their cost-cutting, don't shrink the sales force and marketing budget and then wonder why revenue falls off.

You're hiring whom?

Every leader, without exception, should read Daniel Pink's *Drive*. In it he describes research on how to maximize human performance. What's fascinating about the research is that it turns out that across cultures and economic strata, when the nature of

---

[2] "The Cost of Myopic Management," Natalie Mizik and Robert Jacobson, *Harvard Business Review,* July, 2007.

the work requires brainwork rather than muscle-work, the promise of financial rewards impairs performance. Reliably.

That's right, it impairs it.

This shouldn't be all that surprising, or at least it shouldn't surprise anyone who's watched *National Lampoon's Christmas Vacation*. You might recall that in this little classic, the protagonist, Clark Griswold, becomes furious when he finds out the company he works for isn't going to hand out Christmas bonuses this year.

Clark Griswold isn't the only bonus-eligible employee who puts the money in his mental bank account as soon as the possibility of receiving it is mentioned.

And because these employees have already pocketed the money, from a psychological perspective if it doesn't show up they'll have had money that was theirs taken away from them.

That's robbery, which means that until bonus day they live in fear of being robbed.

The impact of fear on performance is well-understood. Fear gives you the energy you need to climb a tall tree to get away from a bear, even though you're 30 pounds overweight and consider aerobic exercise to be bending over to tie your shoes.

But fear also makes people stupid. There's nothing they or you can do about it. It's how things are. Faced with an enraged bear, even though we've all been told to curl up in a ball and hope the bear loses interest, most of us, once the fear takes hold, will run as fast as we can, which is to say, quite a lot slower than the bear.

The promise of a bonus leads to ongoing fear of not getting it, which inevitably leads to worse performance than if the subject had never come up.

Oh, one more thing: As Alfie Kohn pointed out a very long time ago, when you offer a bonus in exchange for better performance, it's really just a bribe.[3] Should you really have to bribe employees to give you their best work?

As Pink explains in *Drive*, there's a better way to get the best

---

[3] *Punished by rewards: The Trouble with Gold Stars, Incentive Plans, A's, Praise, and Other Bribes,* 1999.

out of people. Offer them *autonomy, mastery,* and *purpose.* That is, give them as much control as possible over what they do; give them the opportunity to perfect skills they personally value; and give them an opportunity to accomplish something important.

Like, for example, the company's mission, and if the mission isn't important, if your company isn't trying to provide important value to society, there's something seriously wrong with your company; namely, nobody is going to have any interest in buying anything from it.

CEO Compensation

Imagine you're hiring a financial analyst. You've gone through the process, winnowed down the candidates to a promising young woman who has all the right skills and background to be successful.

"So," you ask, "what are your expectations with respect to salary?"

"That depends," she answers. "If you want acceptable work, I'll take the job for $90,000 a year plus a 5 percent performance bonus. If you want good work I'll ask you to pay me $100,000 plus a 10 percent bonus. But if you want really spectacular work, that will cost you $125,000 plus a 15 percent bonus."

Do you want to hire someone who indexes the quality of their work to their compensation? This is the exact conversation candidates for the position of CEO have with the board of director's compensation committee in just about every publicly held corporation in America.

The buzz phrase is that boards have to "align incentives" with business goals.

What does this mean? It means boards of directors actively decide to hire CEOs who will only act in the best interests of the company if they're bribed to do so.

Imagine an alternative. The board's conversation with CEO candidates goes like this: "How will you figure out what this company needs to do to profitably grow?" And, "Once you have a clear picture of what it's going to take, what kinds of steps will you take to make it happen?"

And, the board only hires from among the candidates who

clearly want, deep in their guts, the opportunity to build a great company and consider that opportunity to be the most important part of their compensation.

In other words, the board uses the same criteria every supervisor and middle manager uses when hiring, assuming they know how to go about hiring great employees. They look for people who are motivated by achievement. That is, autonomy, mastery, and purpose.

Socialism?

Doesn't sound like capitalism, does it? But, of course, it is capitalism. Adam Smith didn't assume people try to maximize their wealth. His assumption was that people try to maximize "utility," which means everything they value.

Socialists don't argue with this assumption. For all it matters, socialism is an economic system in which government owns the means of production. It's also a bit of invective hurled by the uncouth at those they disagree with. Ignore those who fret about whether your loyal authors are nefariously trying to undermine capitalism in all its glory.

So no, this doesn't mean business leaders get to ignore the company's finances altogether. Companies do, after all, have to operate in the black or they stop being companies and start being acquisition-bait.

What it does mean is that as business leaders set their personal priorities, they think in terms of competitive advantage, of products superior to anything else available, of customer care so amazing customers will feel guilty buying from anyone else.

Cost cutting in the cognitive enterprise

In cognitive enterprises, business leaders still pay close attention to operational efficiency, but with significant differences from how most companies think about the subject today.

First of all, for *cognitive* enterprises there are limits to how much the company is willing to save if the trade-off is doing things dumber. In a cognitive enterprise, effectiveness trumps efficiency. So does excellence, in the sense of the ability to customize, tailor, and generally add more value than customers would get from excessively standardized and commoditized products and services.

Especially among buyers of luxuries, when they ask for something that makes obvious sense and are told, "I'm sorry but that would violate our policy." That's clearly not a good customer-retention tactic.

Effectiveness and excellence beat efficiency. And even when the goal is efficiency, reducing the cost of some business process or other, the bottom-line goal is still different.

Most companies, when they cut costs, expect the reduced operating expense to fall to the bottom line. Those who lead cognitive enterprises, in contrast, use most of their reductions in operating costs to reduce product pricing, which further increases market share, wallet share, and therefore net revenue, giving them more money to reinvest in the business the following year.

Or, they use the money saved for R&D, more advertising, or something else that, in the long run, will help them sell more products to more customers.

Here's something they don't do: artificially shift costs around so they land in this or next fiscal year. They don't do that for two important reasons.

First, and the simplest, shifting costs back and forth across the fiscal year boundary results in financial statements that don't help executives understand how the company is actually doing. It's lying to yourself and believing it, even though you know what you're saying is false.

Cognitive enterprises must be led by executives who insist on understanding the company's performance and what drives it. They'll have no patience for financial statements that have been fiddled with to present an artificially rosy picture.

The second reason is even more important. To understand it, take the popular practice of delaying new hires until after the new fiscal year begins. We could be more diplomatic, but really there are only two possibilities. In the end, filling the position will either make the company more competitive, or it will make it less competitive.

If it will make the company more competitive, filling it earlier will make the company more competitive earlier, which means hiring should be accelerated. If it will make the company less competitive the company shouldn't fill the position ever, because what would be the point?

The one action that never makes sense is delaying the hire. This is just as true for any of the other cost-deferment actions business managers routinely engage in, just to make the books look better than they really are.

Science fiction

Decades from now we finally colonize Mars. Twenty years after the first colonists make the red planet their home they open the first Martian corporation.

Twenty years after that, the last hold-out business on Earth closes its doors, unable to compete with its Martian brethren.

What makes the difference?

Mars' orbit makes its year twice as long as a terrestrial year. As a result Martian corporations have half the number of year-end closings.

It's an insurmountable advantage.

The finale

Here's where we end up:

In the cognitive enterprise, business leaders want all the brains in the enterprise actively engaged in the effort of advancing the mission. Advancing the business model matters too, but, recalling that autonomy, mastery and *purpose* are what get the best performance from the best of the workforce, it's the mission that connects to purpose. And, by focusing everyone on the mission the efforts of individual contributors are more likely to mesh rather than conflict.

There is, after all, a difference between a business staffed with people who are individually smart and a business staffed with people who are both individually smart and in agreement on the fundamentals. It's only in the latter case that the smartness of the individuals who make up the enterprise is additive (or, possibly, multiplicative), which is essential to making the enterprise itself act as if it were smart as well.

Too many employees see their company's top executives taking home as much as 10% of the company's total compensation budget, in exchange for which they play financial games instead of attending to the purpose of the business they're responsible for. When leaders make it clear through their actions and compensation that it's all about the money, employees are less likely to place their focus on accomplishing the company's putative mission.

For executives who focus on the mission while honing the business model, on the other hand (on what the company exists to provide to the larger society it lives in while operating as effectively as possible) the outstanding outcome will be a more profitable and faster-growing business than those of competitors who worry about fine-tuning the profit picture.

The best way to make money is to not worry about the money.[4]

---

[4] Or the split infinitive.

3. Permeability

"There is no them, there's only us!"—U2: Invisible

Canaries in the coal mine
Canary #1

Every January, leaders in the automotive industry gather in Detroit, Michigan to show-off and tout their products for the coming year. The 2015 North American International Auto Show (NAIAS) was no exception as manufacturers attempted to "one-up" each other with dazzling presentations of their new designs to the throngs of industry insiders and analysts. As with all conferences, there is a massive showroom floor where vendors display their wares and a theatre where leaders within the industry make grandiose speeches on a wide range of industry topics.

It's also a networking event, where members of this very special society gather to have "cartalk" and discuss various aspects of the petro-sexual handbook.

It's a classic *us*, not *them* meeting. Outsiders are seldom welcome.

This is why it was particularly unusual to see the ultimate outsider, a Silicon Valley billionaire, giving a speech during one of the sessions.

Yes, Elon Musk, founder of Tesla Motors, electric cars or golf carts as some petro-heads would call them; giving a lecture on the automobile business to those who know everything about it.

Silicon Valley, the gizmo guys lecturing the sultans of industry from Detroit, Tokyo, Munich and Milan. There would no doubt be controversy.

Musk forsook his usual brash style and started with a more humble approach in a moderated question and answer session. His opening remarks set the tone as he explained his mission at the auto show was to strum-up more competition from his more resourceful competitors.

Huh! He was looking for some legitimate competition: Serious investments from the auto manufacturers in the electric cars that weren't ugly, too slow or limited in range.

Musk, or rather Tesla, has a clear vision of the problem it is trying to solve which in a nutshell is the potential damage to the environment caused by millions of petro burning automobiles.

A clear threat to the stay-the-same auto industry built on the internal combustion engine.

Tesla knows that for true transformation to occur within the auto industry, it needs the most resourceful competitors to see a viable market, a compelling economic model and advancements in technology.

And so, Musk made his case claiming that Tesla would sell and build 500,000 electric cars by 2020 and would ramp production to several million units by 2025 with a lower cost, mass market model. He further explained that if Tesla was not reinvesting all of its profits on building a super-charger infrastructure, a dealer network and a gigafactory for improved power generation, it would be profitable under GAAP reporting rules.

What Tesla was saying to the automakers is that there is a market, it's economically viable and we have developed the technology to deliver a differentiated customer experience.

Then Musk offered an olive branch to his long time detractors. He stated Tesla had open-sourced all of its patents and offered its supercharge network to any that wanted to use it.

A playbook right out of Silicon Valley where organizations believe that an open, permeable approach to problem solving creates a rising tide that lifts all boats – a long-term market for true competition.

Tesla knows ultimately it's not its technology that will differentiate it, but its ability to innovate that will help it succeed in the marketplace.

If you don't listen to us, take it from a guy who chose two of the worst industries in which to compete, cars and rockets, where Musk states "if it's important enough to try, then it should be done even if failure is the probable outcome."

Permeability is the new normal.

Canary #2

Consider the case of Apple. In 2010 alone:

Apple forced Chris Ostmo to change the name of his journal-Pad app because, according to Apple's lawyers, this only made sense, on the grounds that "journalPad" infringed on Apple's trademark.

Too bad Apple didn't own the rights to "pad." What it did and does own are the rights to many more lawyers than some poor schmuck app developer.

Also in 2010, Steve Jobs wrote a longish screed explaining his hostility toward Flash. The gist: Flash, being cross-platform, is 100% proprietary. Apple wants all iOS-compliant applications to use open standards, building them with nothing but Apple's proprietary development tools. And they also must make extensive use of Apple's open-standards-based multi-touch interface instead of those tiresome last-generation mice.

The same gestural standards Apple patented were also applied when suing anyone who mimicked them.

Causing, by the way, others to direct an unpatented gesture in Apple's general direction.

An Apple engineer accidentally left an iPhone prototype in a bar, where it just happened to fall into the hands of someone who figured out it was a prototype and not just another iPhone.

The prototype ended up in the hands of Gizmodo's Jason Chen. Apple's lawyers asked him to return it, which he did.

Even so, Apple persuaded the local gendarmes to obtain a search warrant, which they used as an excuse to break down Chen's door and seize his equipment.

As of this writing, Apple has stopped suing competitors for copying its intellectual property and instead is copying their innovations in its new versions of iOS.

Such are the consequences of investing in lawyers instead of your ecosystem.

Canary #3

Current events: A well-known sandwich shop business and its franchisees require employees to sign a non-compete agreement, apparently on the theory that they might take their knowledge of how to assemble a ham and cheese sandwich to a competitor.

A company in the business of teaching music requires its "independent" contractors to sign non-competes as well. In its case, it threatened to withhold payment unless a contractor deleted all student contacts, including contacts the contractor had known socially before joining the music-teaching firm.

As an independent consultant, one of the authors was asked by several clients to sign master services agreements whose terms and conditions included a transfer of ownership of any and all intellectual property used in fulfillment of his consulting work. Had he agreed, on completion of the contract he could no longer have used his pre-existing intellectual property in any future consulting engagements.

In 2013, "inventors" filed approximately 40,000 new applications for software patents, even though there's no chance at all that even a tiny fraction of these represented non-obvious ideas about something new and interesting software can do – the fundamental test of patentability.

For context, in 2013 the total number of patent applications was approximately 287,000, with fewer than 6,300 patent examiners to review them. Also for context, in the section of the United States Consititution that deals with patents and copyrights, neither the term nor the idea that they protect a form of property are even hinted at.

Meanwhile, as of this writing, among the most active areas of innovation in information technology are the cloud, so-called "big data," and cross-platform development environments. Underpinning all of them are an extraordinary level of reliance on open-source technologies, which, in case you aren't fully familiar with the concept, means their terms of use are smartly constructed so as to prevent anyone from ever making them anyone's private, protected intellectual property.

No matter the CEO, the boundary separating what's inside the corporation from what's outside is becoming more and more permeable.

This isn't a problem. It's a constraint, the difference being that people can solve problems. All they can do with constraints is understand them and deal with them.

Or as the business cliché has it, there are no problems, only opportunities. While not always true, it's a good way to understand permeability. Looked at from one angle it's downright distressing. But from a different perspective it opens up a universe of possibilities.

Especially for those leading cognitive enterprises, there's nothing they can do about this increasing permeability, except exploit it to make their enterprise smarter.

To understand how, we first have to understand the three forces driving this trend: The ETG, the rise of open-source everything, and liquid computing.

The ETG

One of the most compelling attributes of the embedded technology generation (ETG) is the rise of the independent worker.

These tech savvy artisans have a fundamentally different attitude toward work than any generation from times past. Or at least, than any generation since the decline of the Guilds so long ago.

First, the rapid pace of change of the technology-laden world in which they live makes them more adaptable to incremental shifts in their domain. In fact, it's their adoption of the technology that increases the pace. The more they get, the more they want.

ETGers are more pliable in accepting technological change as a way of life.

Second, as a class they're highly social through networked communities – not necessarily more intrinsically social than preceding generations, but more social through networked communities. A consequence, for the ETG, regardless of age, shyness is less of an impediment to sociability. One of the ETG's best-known characteristics is the associations its members have because of the social web. Take Facebook, Twitter and Instagram, professional networks hosted by LinkedIn, and personal-interest-based communities like Ravelry (for knitters) BottleTalk (for wine enthusiasts) and Dogster (for dog enthusiasts). For ETGers, having friends they'd never met is both very real and not the least bit strange.

Tip for CEOs of cognitive enterprises

Don't complain or try to stop employees from spending time with their social-web-organized communities on company time.

After all, when they bring their work home with them they don't charge your company for the use of their desk and personal computers.

Not to mention the value of the additional insights they gain from communities they belong to that are relevant to their professions.

With such a rich, community-based online life, for many the question of work/life balance never comes up. ETGers don't separate their personal and professional lives. It's all just life.

Social networks capitalize on these attributes through their "group" functionality where likeminded people can gather to share information that is of interest to the community. And, because news travels fast in the social web, they are more in touch with the "word on the street" as it moves at light speed across their virtual world.

ETGers are adept in their use of the Social Web, which gives them easier and more plentiful avenues for pursuing opportunities as they unfold in near-real time.

And finally, in their lifetime they have witnessed the continuous erosion of employer and employee relationships. They understand that in modern businesses, employees are considered to be fungible commodities that can easily be discarded at the whim of the organization. So they fundamentally have a trust issue with organizations; from the products they market to the jobs they create.

These attributes will have a far-reaching impact on your organization both now and in the future, because whether or not you realize it, the doors of your organization have been kicked wide open for the world to see. When an employee or contractor ends an association with a business they've worked with, they take the knowledge, experience and judgment they've gained with them.

Not to mention the conclusions they've reached about your

company's corporate culture and style, the caliber of the employees they worked with, and the personalities of the managers to whom they reported.

Just as their replacements will bring with them the knowledge, experience, and judgment they've gained during their associations with competitors, not to mention the different cultures, styles and so on they'll be measuring your company against.

The sooner business leaders recognize and embrace this fact, the faster they can take advantage of it.

Today, organizations spend a lot of time and money trying to protect their secrets. Controls such as physical security mechanisms, closed computer networks, secure applications, encrypted file systems and the threat of termination for disloyalty are their tools. And these tools may have worked in the past. But ETGers, immersed in and fully adapted to the age of untethered computing, have made many of these protective habits useless.

Virtual workers have extended the organization to where physical security does not reach. Closed networks have been opened to facilitate highly integrated business solutions, remote workers, and outsourcers. Secure applications have instituted self-service functionality that exposes them to the social web. A scattered workforce with work to do and unforgiving deadlines bypasses encrypted files systems cumbersome corporate content management and knowledge sharing platforms in favor of their easier-to-use, free, and most important unregulated online brethren for collaboration. The threat of termination? Ho hum. I got the job done. Next time I can get it done for your competitor if you prefer.

So far as precious intellectual capital is concerned, the organizations that lay claim to it are already open books in the domains in which they operate.

They're permeable.

And, that's the exact direction your business should be headed. If that isn't clear, ask yourself this: Which has more good ideas in it: Your business, or Earth?

Presumably, with 7 billion inhabitants who don't work for you, Earth wins. Cognitive enterprises have the right attitude about permeability because, being cognitive, they want to constantly expand their fund of knowledge. They'll quite naturally value their access to a wide world of knowledge that's there for the asking.

It's the companies that best exploit this knowledge – that take full advantage of the business ecosystem in which they operate – that will win. And because they recognize the value of their ecosystem, they'll foster its health and well-being.

Open. Honest. Collaborative. These are the watchwords of the cognitive enterprise. Why? Because openness, honesty and collaboration are the hallmarks of healthy team dynamics, and as Douglas Merrill once said, in a team "all smarter than any of us," unlike a group or committee, where we're all stupider than even the dumbest among us.

To drill down on the importance of collaboration, reference the book, *Value Networks and the True Nature of Collaboration.*

www.mkpress.com/VN

The difference between a group and a team is, in miniature, the difference between an industrial and cognitive enterprise.

The independent workforce has a natural affinity with organizations that are open, honest and collaborative. Want hard evidence? At the moment it's sketchy. For every Tesla that shares its discoveries to improve its whole industry there are a dozen Apples that consider "Not Invented Here" to be their guiding principle. But keep an eye on lists of top employers. The best tend to embrace an open culture.

Tesla embraces openness while generating enormous amounts of intellectual property. In our opinion it serves as an excellent example of a company that successfully walks the delicate tightrope that both separates and connects permeability and discretion.

It's one reason we forecast Tesla's long-term success and even longer-term impact.

Open Source is not software!

Let's talk about the Wild West of intellectual property, the world of open source.

What is open source? First: Open source isn't Linux in the same way rectangles aren't squares. Second, open source isn't only about software, although the number of software packages businesses rely on that are open source is on the increase.

Open source is, first and foremost, a culture – one where creative talent whose location isn't just unknown, it hardly matters – that has loosely banded together. In the words of Eric Raymond, godfather of the open source movement, they've banded together to scratch a personal itch. Open source is cultural norm for many of the people you're hiring.

In one sense open source is a form of protest against the increasingly restrictive and often ridiculous intellectual property laws that exist to protect creative works. For the most part those who participate in open source projects do so for the joy of being creative and sharing the results of their creativity.

Which is to say, Wikipedia has as much in common with bake sales as it does with the *Encyclopedia Britannica*. It's a result of a culture based on sharing intellectual property by making it available for use and community-driven improvement while still preserving some basic rights of authorship.

The open source culture – a culture with equal parts of personal itch-scratching, the joy of creation, and a desire to share or show off – is a driving force behind the success of the social web.

Most of the creative talent your organization will hire has a fundamental connection to the open source culture. Their connection might not be labeled "open source." But not only software and *Wikipedia,* but music, videos, recipes, templates and millions of other creative artifacts are just as much a part of the open source culture as Linux.

The next time someone sends you a YouTube link, before you click on it take a moment to reflect: The enjoyment you're about to get is the result of the open source culture.

And every day, whether you know it or not, as they go about their work, your most creative talent willingly takes from and adds to open source knowledge pools. It's fundamental to their nature and your organization has little control over it.

In case the point isn't clear: Just as your company is a community, every member of your workforce belongs to other communities as well. Each of them has its own open-source body of knowledge. Most members of your workforce, and emphatically those who are ETGers at heart, know that compared to their relationship with your company, their relationships with the communities of interest they belong to are more durable.

When ETGers need to solve a problem or figure something out they look to the social web. Why? It's how they've been doing it their whole lives. Their knowledge sources are Google (sorry, Bing and Yahoo), *Wikipedia,* and whichever website hosts the discussion groups they read and participate in.

They're open, easy to use, have billions of contributors and best of all, they're free. And their embedded knowledge bases continuously grow because whether for vanity, a sincere desire to be of service or the simple joy of creation, members of the ETG contribute knowledge as they seek recognition among their peers.

Industrial-era CEOs dislike the time their ETG workforce spends on the social web during work hours, and worry about their company's intellectual capital leaking through it to their competitors. Wise CEOs worry, instead, that their 20th-century workforce might not know how to tap into this enormous source of free and useful knowledge.

Tesla: Exploiting Permeability

Go back to the difference between mission and business

model introduced in the chapter on finance, and apply it to Tesla. Elon Musk, Tesla's founder and CEO, wants to reduce our carbon footprint, starting with the automobile. That's Tesla's mission, not its business model. It involves designing and building brilliant cars wealthy people will not just *want* to buy but *desire.*

Musk knows that while a single upstart startup company can succeed with his business model, he won't be able to make a dent in his company's mission. So he's chosen instead to use Tesla to develop and prove that technology and business models can both work.

He opened Tesla's patents for the entire automotive industry to use, figuring that whatever value Tesla loses from donating its patents to the ecosystem it will more than make up from the additional innovation, and faster innovation, these free patents will trigger.

And all the other automobile manufacturers who are able to shift their fleets away from internal combustion engines because they have access to these patents will help Tesla accomplish its mission.

That's something true leaders do. They lay a path for others to follow.

Also, Musk probably knows Tesla is just as permeable as any other company. Its technology would have seeped through the cracks into its competitors anyway. After all, many of its engineers are ETGers. On top of which is the nature of innovation itself. In the long run it isn't protectable, because protectable innovations trigger another round, which isn't "protectable."

Mostly, Musk recognized that Tesla must raise the competency of its competitors or electric cars will remain a curiosity in the automotive marketplace. So long as they are, Tesla's ability to sell cars will be limited for the simple reason that electric car buyers need charging stations, just as buyers of gasoline-fueled cars need gas stations. Charging stations are an important part of Tesla's ecosystem. Electric cars have to reach critical mass to encourage entrepreneurs to open them, or for existing gas stations to add electricity to the products they sell.

Expanding this ecosystem isn't altruism. It's enlightened self-interest.

Will this work? While the plural of anecdote is not data,[5] the Chevy Bolt, a longer range electric vehicle announced at a recent Detroit Auto Show, surely constitutes, if not data, at least an indicative data point.

Apple: Resisting Permeability

Contrast Tesla and Apple. Apple has defined itself as a closed organization that routinely tries to control its intellectual property, up to and including applying for a patent for a using a rectangle with rounded edges as the shape for a display device. Astonishingly, the patent was granted, even though the application was filed in 2010, three years after Amazon released its Kindle e-Reader, a display device with rounded edges.

Apple's iOS design language does predate Google's Android solution by a couple of years, and early versions of Android functioned more like Blackberry, the incumbent leader of the time. So the timeline and circumstances would suggest that Google copied Apple's design language.

But Android is an open source software project and the developer community started to shift the user interface look and feel toward iOS functionality, especially for applications that operated on both platforms. Hence; developers took Android in the direction of iOS.

It was the culture of the development community that shaped the future of Android and not some corporate espionage. Google just followed the developers.

By now, Android is the more important innovator for design and functionality, bypassing Apple, which has started to be the imitator.

It's a classic example of how ETGers impact impermeable organizations.

Apple became permeable the moment it allowed outside developers to contribute content to its proprietary devices, and for that matter the moment an Apple programmer took a job someplace else. Steve Jobs recognized the situation but reached the exact opposite conclusion from the one Elon Musk arrived at.

---

[5] The source of this little gem is, sadly, unknown. Call it an open source aphorism.

Innovation builds on itself in an endless loop, so while the Apple design philosophy became a standard within the developer community, which regularly consumes and contributes to open source knowledge pools such as GitHub or the Android project, it turned into an evolving standard whose development is driven by a community that's beyond the control of any one corporation.

Which is how Google and its hardware partners routinely outpace Apple with functional updates. Apple relies solely on its workforce. Google relies on its ecosystem.

Netflix goes both one better. It held a competition for a "collaborative filtering algorithm," open only to *anyone not connected with it,* awarding a million-dollar prize to the winners. It also publishes its current and planned systems architectures in a freely available blog.

Permeable or Permeable by Design

Organizations that are permeable by design will outperform competitors that are only permeable because their attempts at impermeability fail.

Is your business permeable? Yes. You have no choice in the matter. You might as well take advantage of it.

An organization is a group of persons structured to achieve an intended outcome. More and more members of the group will either be ETGers or will develop ETG-like characteristics through osmosis. They'll bring with them their open, informal, and collaborative approach to life, inside and outside their professional situations. This will spread, for two reasons.

The first reason is that when cultures come into contact with each other, their boundaries tend to blur. The second reason is that ETGers' willingness to take advantage of the knowledge of their outside community affiliations gives then a natural advantage over colleagues who suffer from the "Not Invented Here" syndrome.

Eventually, their colleagues will want the same advantage.

That's what Tesla does. Google too. Both are for-profit organizations and trailblazers for others to follow. They embrace the give and take nature of permeability. While talent is their lifeblood, their culture of permeability is what oxygenates it.

It's a world soon to be dominated by ETGers who understand that improvisation, innovation, and their progenitor, imitation, are key differentiators, and that they have no choice but to contribute and consume knowledge within their ecosystem.

Attrition – emigration and immigration might be better terms – ensures their talent will enhance their ecosystems and themselves; emigration by feeding the ecosystem; immigration from harvesting it. Soon this process will be considered a natural part of operating an organization.

Leaders of cognitive enterprises know the open source culture is here to stay. It will lead to new innovations in tools and processes to perform their work. Permeability is about collaboration, but isn't limited to it. In the end, it's about supporting a healthy ecosystem and opening the organization to new ideas.

The workspace is everywhere!

By the first quarter of 2013, laptop makers such as Dell, HP and Lenovo saw a significant decrease in demand for traditional computing devices – laptops and desktops. The demand dropped so much that many industry analysts declared the PC to be dead.

This analysis is, to be charitable, shallow. Demand for traditional PCs is flat for two straightforward reasons: (1) PCs aren't becoming more powerful in ways users care about, so new capabilities aren't generating demand; and (2) most people (and the workforce in most companies) already have the PCs they need.

When everyone has what they need, sales are mostly replacement machines. Of course sales are going to be flat.

But while PCs are far from dead, the reality for them is no less depressing, because in a deep and fundamental way, PCs have become boring. Tablets, smartphones, and wearable computing gadgets are where the action is when it comes to innovative features and uses.

Start with the typical ETG attitude that there is no "work/life balance" – there's just life. With this perspective, and with multiple types of untethered computing devices at their disposal, a specific role is coming into focus for each of these device categories: Smartphones are for on-the-go collaboration, PCs are for serious work, and tablets are mostly for entertainment and lightweight editing and revision.

Multi-device manufacturers such as Apple have picked up on this trend and are delivering a handoff feature where data and activities move seamlessly from device to device. Microsoft and Google have similar solutions in the pipeline.

This functionality is significant and provides the foundation for what's being called "liquid computing," the ability to start an activity in one place on one device and resume it on another. It's fluid and operates without all of the nonsense of managing master records, bookmarks and breakpoints to keep track of what you're doing.

This ability has far reaching implications into the world of enterprise workflow, process integrity and data security. Imagine a worker starting a business transaction such as a sales order on his/her desktop at work, then resuming it on the train ride home on his/her tablet or mobile phone, all without interruption.

Liquid computing will make the workspace not just ubiquitous, but seamless.

And it makes the enterprise even more permeable. Couple liquid computing with the open source culture of your creative staff and it's even easier for people who aren't your employees to contribute to your projects.

Putting it all together

You have a stark choice. You can embrace the permeability of your organization and gain the speed and cost advantages permeability has to offer. Or, you can engage in a futile effort to fight it.

You can surf the wave or, like the legendary King Canute, try to keep the tide from coming in.

Investing in futility is rarely a good idea.

The bottom-line lesson here is that all enterprises are part of an "ecosystem." Cognitive enterprises will invest in the health of the ecosystems they operate in, knowing that, fertilizer analogies notwithstanding, they'll get more out of their investment than they put into it.

Sorry about the mixed metaphors.

4. The decline of metrics

"It ain't what you don't know that gets you into trouble. It's what you know for sure that just ain't so."— Mark Twain

Canaries in the coal mine

Canary #1

Once upon a time there was a team of consultants. A process re-engineering team. They promised their client measurable improvements, and the client was glad to have this assurance of tangible improvement.

And so the re-engineering team got to work. They installed imaging and workflow technologies. They drew swim-lane diagrams. They measured the baseline cycle time for the end-to-end process they were going to improve, which turned out to be about three days: The process began when an insurance application form arrived in the mailroom and finished when the underwriters had finished processing the application.

The project was a spectacular success: Cycle time plummeted, from the original three days to a mere half day.

Nonetheless, the underwriters complained. The consultants chalked up their complaints to the natural resistance all employees have to all changes, and brought out their statistical analysis of before and after cycle times.

It was undeniable: Cycle time had improved, and improved dramatically, not by just an increment.

And yet, the underwriters continued to complain. The problem, they explained was that with the old system they could spread the application forms and supporting material across their desks, looking at whatever they needed to look at in whatever sequence they needed to look at it.

But with the new system they could only look at one page of one form at a time on their computer screens. This made underwriting much slower than it used to be.

And yet, overall cycle time had improved, so the underwriters were advised to live with the inconvenience.

Which was too bad, because it turned out that while cycle time had improved, and improved dramatically, underwriting was the bottleneck step in the end-to-end process. What the re-engineering team didn't realize was that while speeding up non-bottleneck steps and slowing down bottleneck steps might improve cycle time, it damages throughput – an independent measure of process speed.

In this case, underwriting time had roughly doubled, from one hour per underwriter per application to two, which meant process throughput, and therefore capacity was reduced from about eight policies per underwriter per day to only four policies per underwriter per day.

The first moral of this story is that, when consultants promise measureable improvements, that's fine, so long as their clients insist on being the ones to decide which metrics should be improved, and by extension which ones can't be made worse.

The second moral is an inviolable rule of metrics, which is that anything you don't measure you don't get.

That leaves one more moral: When discussing terms with a process re-engineering consulting group, make sure to ask this critical question: "Show me the engineer."

Canary #2

One of your loyal authors once worked for an industry association – one prominent in the printing industry. A service we'd been asked to provide our members was to collect and publish industry benchmarks.

We formed a committee composed of some smart folks from various printers and set about our task.

Shortly thereafter we abandoned it.

The problem wasn't that we couldn't figure out what to measure. That was straightforward: Printers care about waste and productivity – how many bad copies have to be thrown out and how many good copies per hour they produce.

No, the problem, we discovered, was that no two printers have exactly the same goals.

A company that prints an ultra-high-quality magazine like

National Geographic is going to have a lot more waste than one that prints a news-weekly like *Time* because the art directors responsible for the advertisements printed in magazines are going to be far more finicky when their ad appears in *National Geographic* than in *Time.*

Although offsetting this is that newsweeklies use cheaper paper that's more likely to break during a press run.

A company that specializes in smaller publications with shorter print runs will have more waste as a percentage of total production than ones with long print runs, because most waste occurs as the press is coming up to speed from a standing start.

Book printers, at least those that print only in black and white, will have less waste than magazine printers that print in color, because black and white doesn't require tuning the color balance.

Newspapers care about print quality, but not to the extent magazine printers do – they don't have art directors looking over their shoulders. What they do have is a less-forgiving production schedule and cheaper paper that breaks more easily, which has a significant impact on waste.

Then there's the question of end point. Four-color printing involves an oven to dry the inks. Book printing happens in "signatures" – blocks of pages – that are then fed into a separate operation called the bindery, after which they're fed into another, separate operation where the cover is put on.

Newspapers ... at least the Sunday paper ... are fed into a mailroom operation where the advertising inserts are put in.

And so on.

By the time we'd looked at all the variations we figured out we'd need thousands of participants in order to develop benchmarks that would be of any use to our members. Which was too bad, because there weren't that many printing companies to provide the raw data we'd have needed to calculate them.

Most businesses have access to industry benchmarks. The question is, is the printing industry uniquely complicated when it comes to comparisons? Or is the desire for (and revenue to be derived from) publishing benchmarks so intense that minor matters like providing valid comparisons is too unimportant to overshadow it?

Canary #3

In 2014, a scandal at the Veterans Administration hit the front pages.

The scandal wasn't that the VA was providing awful care to veterans. Veteran satisfaction with VA care was, if not wonderful, at least on a par with private-sector care. An acquaintance who heads a chapter of the Vietnam Veterans Association and was involved in the current inquiry confirmed that care quality wasn't, for the most part, an issue.

Just as telling, nobody in the VA delayed care or treatment. Veterans seeking care were scheduled into the earliest timeslots available.

The scandal was that managers throughout the VA required staff to fudge the numbers to make it appear the agency was meeting its required service levels.

The VA's leaders, from General Shinseki on down, extended organizational metrics to individuals. It's a common mistake, usually associated with the need to hold employees accountable (see Chapter 9).

What was true for Jeff Skilling and Ken Lay at Enron turned out to be just as true for low-level managers at the VA. When your performance is gauged by numbers, you have an incentive to fudge the numbers, which in turn makes the numbers useless for gauging organizational performance.

Which brings us to the most astonishing aspect of this whole sorry mess. General Shinseki apparently acted like a manager, not like a leader, and not a very good manager, either.

Shinseki relied on reports, his 12-level chain of command, and extensive time spent with the VA's regional medical directors, none of whom mentioned the metrics-fudging. Why would anyone expect them to?

Generals are supposed to understand that if they want to know what's really going on, they need to talk to the soldiers. There were no indications Shinseki did much of this.

Look, fudging management reports to make performance look better is a time-honored tradition in the world of organizational dynamics. This isn't a scandal in any meaningful sense of the word.

If there's a scandal, it's that the metric that mattered most, a metric on which lives depend if it's the VA, was jeopardized by the insistence on measuring individual performance. That metric? Demand per unit of Capacity. So long as it's less than one day to cover day-to-day variations in demand, veterans, or in your case your customers, will get the care they need when they need it.

Turns out, in the VA, along with many customer service call centers, it was nowhere close.

Canary #4

In the old days of programmers who did nothing but write code, there were plenty of attempts to measure programmer productivity. They had one thing in common: They failed. Miserably.

Some managers counted lines of code. This had only a few problems: (1) the best programmers accomplish the same task with the fewest lines of code; (2) the moment programmers knew they were being measured this way they added lines of code that did nothing but take up space and got counted as another line of code the programmer had written; (3) it penalized programmers who used languages that accomplished more with the same number of lines of code.

Then someone invented the "function point," a standard unit of program functionality. Function points were terrific, except for a few problems of their own, like, for example, (1) different languages let programmers deliver the same number of function points with dramatically different levels of effort; and (2) just try to explain to anyone interested in the business in how hard it might be to achieve their goals on a computer that "this task will require 47 function points."

Response: "What does a function point look like?"

Response to response: "Well, it doesn't actually look like anything – it's kind of a theoretical construct."

And so on. In spite of at least four decades of trying, efforts to create reliable ways to measure programmer productivity have all fizzled.

And now, it's become even more pointless, because modern application development methodologies require developers to spend lots of time interacting informally with business managers and users, talking about what they need systems to do, how closely their current iteration is to doing it. All this would need to count toward programmer productivity were we still to try to measure it.

Programmer productivity measurement after four decades, is nothing but failure.

Seems like a perfect opportunity to give up.

The defining metric of business punditry is sufficiency of quotation – the extent to which attribution to the pundit settles the matter in question.

Which is how, in spite of Peter Drucker's prodigious positive impact on modern business practice, the negative impact of a single quote might well overshadow all of his good work.

The quote: "If you can't measure you can't manage." Call it Drucker's Metrics Dictum. It's a true enough statement, but it ignores two corollaries:

Corollary #1: If you can measure, most likely you still can't manage.

Corollary #2: If you mis-measure, you'll mismanage.

Corollary #1: If you can measure, most likely you still can't manage

Imagine you're running a company, and you decide it's important to grow year-over-year revenue. You would, of course, be right.

So you collect your executive team and put a revenue growth plan together. It entails product enhancements, better customer care, a shiny new advertising campaign, and value-based pricing.

And, you fire the old sales manager and replace him with someone more aggressive.

Everyone does what they're supposed to do, including you: You measure revenue, on the grounds that if you can't measure you can't manage, and revenue does, in fact, increase.

The Metrics ROI Conundrum

Regardless of the type of metric, whether SMART goals, Key Performance Indicators (KPIs), Balanced Scorecard, or even the use of standard financial ratios, presumably these gauge systems and processes that have to be managed.

Which brings up the question: Are there any metrics that demonstrate that the value of using metrics exceeds the investment required to produce them?

Developing a metric like this is, as your high school math textbooks used to say, left as an exercise for the reader.

Being possessed of some intellectual depth you also insist on some additional metrics. Your product manager uses focus groups to assess how much better your company's new products are than their predecessors. Customer service uses automated follow-up surveys to make sure customers who make use of the contact center are happy with the service they receive. You engage a market research firm to gauge reactions to your new advertising campaign, and also to determine how your products' pricing compares to the marketplace. And, your new sales manager is quite happy to report year-over-year statistics for sales production.

The metrics all come out well, and so you conclude the program worked. Champagne and bonuses all around!

Except that no, you can't draw that conclusion, for three reasons:

- The economy this year was much stronger than last year.
- One of your competitors went out of business, and another abandoned your marketplace.
- Sales of two of your "legacy products" that have been on the market for several years and received no special attention grew more than the new and improved ones.

You measured, and you learned. What, exactly? You know you did well but you don't know why, which means you don't know whether your success was the result of a good plan or dumb luck.

Which in turn means you have no useful guidance for what you should do next year to build on this year's momentum.

Here's what Drucker should have said: "If you can't model you can't manage." A model in this context describes the cause-and-effect relationships connecting the factors that drive business success – the business model from Chapter 3.

Good quantitative models have a few characteristics: (1) They aren't overly simplistic. They include every factor that might have a significant impact on success; (2) they also aren't overly complex. They don't include so many factors that nobody can make sense of them; (3) they're testable. There's a way to collect evidence and analyze it to determine whether or not the model works, and if it doesn't how to modify it so it does; and (4) they're mostly imaginary entities that don't exist here on the planet we like to call Earth.

Okay, that isn't entirely fair. It is possible to construct and test a rigorous model of some businesses.[6] What gets in the way is the shrinking stay-the-same to change ratio. By the time a business has finished constructing, testing, and adequately refining its model, the model it has will be of the business it used to be, operating in the marketplace as it used to be.

Which isn't to say there's no hope and the best you can do is manage your business by whim and gut feel. Far from it. What it does mean is that from the perspective of understanding how your business works there are times when qualitative models will just have to do, an example of a qualitative model being, "If we take care of our customers they'll come back and bring their friends."

So the best you can hope for with respect to traditional metrics is that they can serve as evidence, not proof, that your business model does or doesn't work the way you think it does.

Which, to be fair, is useful information when you're trying to make a sustainable profit.

It isn't too far off to say the starting point for making an enterprise cognitive is this sort of modeling, and at all levels of the organization. It's by understanding the levers and buttons that

---

[6] If you're interested, Google "value driver analysis."

managers can pull and push to make success happen that an enterprise can cognitively assess its alternatives and choose from among them.

What you can't manage if you can't measure

As is so often the case, the problem with Drucker's Metrics Dictum isn't that it's always invalid. Quite the opposite – the problem is that it's valid just often enough to create the false impression that it's always valid.

Take a manufacturing line, the construct around which so many of the business concepts challenged in this book are built. When you're manufacturing something, you want to avoid defects – out-of-specification products that, if sold, will generate returns and high repair costs if you're lucky, and fatalities if you are unlucky.

Defects are a bad thing. If you can't detect them, count them, and quantify them, you can't properly manage your factory. The same may be said of all the other standard production-line metrics: Fixed costs, incremental costs, cycle time, and throughput.

You don't need models here. You need to know if you have problems and if so, where in the manufacturing process they're coming from. You need to know this so you can avoid selling defective products, and improve the process so you don't keep on manufacturing defective products.

What you can't manage even if you can measure

Everything that isn't a manufacturing process.

Corollary #2: If you mis-measure you'll mismanage

Metrics drive behavior. It isn't too extreme to say that this, much more than understanding how your business is doing, is the reason for establishing them. Whether or not you agree doesn't matter, because while using metrics to understand how your business is doing is optional, their impact on behavior is not.

Which leads to the first rule of business metrics: You get

what you measure – that's the risk you take.

Here's how this risk plays out.

The four metrics fallacies: When businesses set out to measure things, they often fall prey to one or more of these four mistakes – call them the four metrics fallacies:

- Measuring the right things but measuring them wrong.
- Measuring the wrong things, whether they're measured right or wrong.
- Failing to measure something important.
- Extending measures to individual employees.

The first two fallacies are pretty obvious. Measure something wrong and employees will deliver whatever outcomes result in the metric looking better. Measure the wrong thing and even if you hit the bull's-eye, when employees make that metric look better their achievements will, at best, be irrelevant to business progress.

How businesses end up with the wrong metrics: These mistakes are sadly common. Businesses usually make them when someone asks, "What metrics should we use for this?"

Because having been asked, someone is bound to try to answer the question, sometimes in the form of another question: What metrics do other companies use for this?

There's no recovering from these questions, other than to stop the conversation in its tracks, perhaps by running from the room screaming, because these are horribly wrong questions.

They're wrong because they violate the first rule of design, which, as expressed by the great architect Louis Sullivan, is _form follows function._

The place to start isn't what metrics you should use. The place to start is to understand your goals, stated in plain language. Once you understand your goals you can devise metrics to determine whether you're achieving them or not. But if you start with the metric you're skipping the part about deciding what's important.

And if you start by asking what metrics other companies use you're substituting their goals for your goals.

Or, even worse, you might start by deciding to compare

yourself to industry benchmarks – averages of a metric designed by a committee that might or might not have anything to do with the goals of any of the organizations contributing data to it (Canary #2).

"What metric should we use" guarantees you'll run afoul of one of the first two metrics fallacies.

But that's fixable. What isn't fixable is metrics fallacy #3. Because metrics drive behavior, you get what you measure, which also means **anything you don't measure you don't get**.

What don't you measure? In the case of most businesses, you don't measure what's either complicated or expensive to measure, which usually works out to be everything that matters most.

What matters most depends on your business model, of course, but let's keep it simple. In most businesses the list of what matters most looks something like this:

- *Product competitiveness:* How well your products stand up to the competition. How can you tell? The usual tools are focus groups and marketplace surveys. Hold that thought.
- *Customer satisfaction and loyalty:* The extent to which your customers are likely to come back and bring their friends. How can you tell? Marketplace surveys. Continue to hold that thought.
- *Employee enthusiasm and (sorry!) engagement:* How much energy, creativity, initiative, and plain hard work employees bring to their efforts on your behalf. How can you tell? That's right, surveys.

This isn't the place for a long tirade about focus groups. Instead, two words: New Coke. Now a few more, because the New Coke retelling isn't always accurate. What went wrong with New Coke wasn't that a bunch of dimwitted marketeers couldn't figure out what was obvious to everyone else. What went wrong with New Coke was that the market tests were based on quantities suitable for sipping – small Dixie cups. Cola drinkers who sipped New Coke liked it. The problem is that when most people drink a can of cola they don't sip. They quaff. They gulp. They take big swallows because they're hot and thirsty.

The folks at Coca Cola didn't figure this out until way too late in the game, but in their defense it was an easy mistake to make.

Easy enough that it's easy to imagine someone putting together focus groups to assess other products making equivalent mistakes.

Surveys

There was a time when many consumers were excited to participate in surveys. Participating in a survey meant having some influence over the course of events.

But then came the push poll, where companies more interested in publicizing survey results than learning from them discovered they could easily manipulate poll results by how they phrase the question (old, old example from the fast-food burger wars: A Burger King poll that asked, "Which would you rather eat – a disgusting, greasy hockey-puck-shaped disk of fried ground beef or a delicious, flame-broiled hamburger?")

At about the same time, marketing executives figured they couldn't be blamed for failures if they based their decisions on polling or survey data, and so the sheer number of polls increased.

And so, fewer and fewer consumers were willing to donate their time to pollsters.

Meanwhile, the Internet happened and with it online surveys. These are much less expensive to administer and tabulate than telephone polling. As a result they've become increasingly popular, even though here's what everyone knows who uses these things: There's only one way to persuade consumers to participate in an online survey and that's to promise a reward, usually entry into a drawing for something valuable, like an iPad or two one-way tickets to Mozambique.

The problem: Consumers are just as likely to win if they simply click "1" in response to every question as if they respond honestly and thoughtfully. The quantitative data collected from Internet surveys is just about 100% worthless. The only data worth looking at lies in the written comments, which don't lend themselves to statistical analysis.

This is why such metrics as the Net Promoter Index, no matter how well-intentioned, are questionable. Employee surveys suffer from parallel challenges, as anyone knows who has participated in one.

Bottom line: Even if you try to measure what's most important in your business, it's highly likely you won't be able to trust the results.

But on the other hand, if you fail to measure product competitiveness but do measure other business attributes that more-easily lend themselves to data collection ... like the defect rate, manufacturing throughput, and cost of raw materials ... you won't get competitive products, because once you start measuring something, anything you don't measure you don't get.

Similarly, if, in your customer service call center you collect the usual metrics, like queue time, abandon rate, and call time but don't measure what's hard to measure – did the call center agent resolve the caller's issue in a way that maximizes the likelihood of that customer coming back and bringing friends along – you'll get short calls that fix nothing.

How to measure employee enthusiasm, initiative, and engagement

Ever watch the show *Undercover Boss*?

It shows bosses who have been relying on management reports and their chains of command to understand the working conditions in their companies and how employees are reacting to them.

It turns out these are, for the most part, decent folks who just trusted the wrong information sources. Once they got out into their organizations to see things firsthand they got an entirely different picture of things.

It's management by walking around in a disguise.

The three limitations to this technique:

- It's time-consuming, even in the show, where the boss only sees a few areas of the company firsthand.
- You'll only understand what's going on in those parts of the company you see first-hand – you won't be getting a representative sample.
- It requires access to a top-notch make-up artist.

True story: An HR consultant, engaged to assist with development of sound HR metrics, recommended employee turnover as a useful metric. To which one of the company's managers asked, shouldn't the metric be undesired turnover instead?

The answer was telling: The consultant explained that in his experience the difference between the two numbers would be too small to worry about. Which betrayed total ignorance of the first rule of metrics, because it doesn't matter whether the two metrics would be within a few decimal places of each other. What mattered, and continues to matter, is the behavior each metric drives. Measure turnover and managers will no longer terminate even their worst employees.

Which brings us to metrics fallacy #4: Extending metrics to individual employees. Start with measuring undesired turnover. Do this, and use the results to assess individual managers, and the result will be completely predictable: No matter who resigns, the manager will solemnly swear the employee was a colossal pain in the neck and the company is better off without them.

More generally, extend any metric to individual managers, employees, or even to teams, and you can predict the result with ease. Whoever is being measured will do everything they can to game it, whether they live in the executive suite, middle-managerial offices, or employee cubicles.

What makes a useful system of metrics

Here's what's needed to put together a useful system of metrics. A good system of metrics must be connected, consistent, calibrated, complete, communicated, and current. Call it the *Six C's*. In order:

- **Connected:** Good metrics are connected to important goals. In fact, this states the relationship backward. Good metrics begin as important goals, stated in English. Then you convert the English to Math to arrive at the metric.
- **Consistent:** Consistent metrics always go in one direction when the situation improves and the other direction when the situation deteriorates. Consistency is important because you get what you measure – that's the whole point. So, if good,

doesn't always point in one direction and bad in the other, what you'll get is a lot of action whose impact on the business can't be predicted.

- This is the biggest problem with the Total Cost of Ownership (TCO) measures so popular in the IT industry – they aren't consistent. Some of the actions you might take to lower TCO make your situation worse (eliminating training, for example); others improve your situation (standardizing server configurations). Because it's a cost measure, everyone will assume lower is better, sometimes to the detriment of your business.

- *Calibrated:* Calibration means whoever records the value of a measure, in the same situation the measure will take on the same value. It also means the data that underlie the measure are free from sample bias and other data quality problems. It means that you can count on the numbers themselves.

- *Complete:* You'll recall that anything you don't measure you don't get. Hence any useful system of measures must be complete. It must include all of the factors that are important to business success.

- *Communicated:* Metrics serve two, and only two, purposes. They let you know how well your organization is working, and they drive behavior to get it to work better. If you don't communicate the results, you'll know how well your organization is working and that will be the end of the benefit.

- *Current:* Goals change. Establishing appropriate metrics and setting up systems to collect and analyze the data necessary to provide them takes time and effort. The temptation to be lazy and make do with the reports you have instead of replacing them with new reports appropriate to the new goals is significant. Don't succumb.

What's the problem?

Avoid the metrics fallacies, make sure your metrics follow the 6 C's formulation, and it's all good.

Does it have to be this complicated?
Yes. To understand why, look no further than your account-

ing system.

GAAP accounting is nothing more than a time-tested metrics system. It doesn't conform to some of the 6Cs. By itself it isn't Complete (hence the interest in balanced scorecards).

Often, it isn't Current, as keeping the chart of accounts in sync with the business can be a challenge.

On the other hand, compared to any other metric you might institute, those reported by your accounting system have been explored in depth for centuries and are staggeringly well understood.

So think about what's required to implement a good accounting system. There's no reason to expect the effort to implement any other system of metrics should be any less expensive, time-consuming, and labor-intensive, for a couple of reasons.

The first: Metrics aren't free. They don't just require a reporting system. They must be integrated into your operational systems. Otherwise, someone will have to push numbers into a separate reporting system after the real work gets done. They'll have to get those numbers from somewhere, and if it isn't from your operational systems that somewhere will come down to manual data-collection and entry, with all the error-proneness and delays that suggests.

The second: Metrics also aren't immediate. They take time to develop and fine-tune. In the industrial age that was just fine. It still would be if it weren't for that pesky stay-the-same to change ratio. Now, there's a good chance that by the time you've developed a full system of useful metrics, they'll be rolled out just in time to point everyone's behavior in the wrong direction.

What metrics are for

What executives and managers want from a system of metrics is based on Drucker's Metrics Dictum. They're looking for a way to know What's Going On Out There. For management, metrics is an organizational listening channel, right alongside management by walking around, an open-door policy, "skip lunches" (where executives have lunch with line employees, skipping layers of the management hierarchy) and so on.

In principle, they ought to be able to use the management hierarchy for organizational listening and have done with it. In practice, in most organizations every node in the management hierarchy carefully orchestrates the flow of information so that what everyone in it most needs to know is what's carefully cleansed, scrubbed, sanded down, and otherwise sanitized so they won't worry their pretty little heads about things.

Because enough managers either shoot the messenger or hold people accountable, nobody with a brain is foolish enough to give his or her manager any unvarnished bad news.

Whatever else you do, fight this tendency. Want a cognitive enterprise? It starts with the shared attitude of wanting to understand how things work and how things are working.

Call it a culture of honest inquiry. From the perspective of organizational listening it's essential, if for no other reason than that you have to be able to rely on your management hierarchy. Yes, have to, because all of the person-to-person alternatives just don't scale very well.

If you're an entrepreneur with fifty employees, walking around and talking with everyone is all you need to do to know What's Going On Out There. If you used to be an entrepreneur until success happened, and you now have thousands of employees, good luck with that. The management hierarchy is how you partition responsibilities so everyone knows what their current area of focus is supposed to be. Among the reasons you need one is that your brain doesn't scale well enough to personally manage everything that happens in every part of the company.

By the same token your ability to listen to everyone in every part of the company also doesn't scale. The management hierarchy should help you out for organizational listening just as it does for directing traffic. And it can, but only if you create an environment that encourages it.

Metrics is another organizational listening channel among many. It's also a channel you can use to explain what you consider to be important, which is, in fact, how metrics drives behavior. When you let employees know what you're measuring, you're telling them what you consider to be important, and, by extension, what you don't.

So metrics do drive behavior. Regrettably, as explained at

length in this chapter, more often than not metrics drive the wrong behavior because of the enormous difficulty and effort required to construct a useful system of metrics and keep it up to date.

Sometimes, especially in a manufacturing environment, metrics can be a useful tool in gaining this understanding – not when used in isolation but when coupled with other, complementary techniques.

For some time to come, the stay-the-same to change ratio won't be so small that metrics are completely useless. But when metrics turn out to be the wrong tool of the job, abandon them without regret.

When you don't – when you're confident your metrics will drive desirable behavior, by all means continue using them. But, supplement metrics with other techniques, like walking around, talking to employees and customers, and, more to the point, listening to them. Such interactions also tell employees what management is paying attention to.

Do this and you just might be surprised at how well you'll find you can manage.

Analytics are the new metrics

Analytics are the new metrics.

The drive to establish metrics was, in an important sense, valuable. It was built around the idea that decisions should be driven by evidence – the more objective and quantitative, the better.

But as should be clear by now, developing good metrics and the systems needed to produce them are neither quick nor cheap. And while they can be useful for answering the question, "How did we do?" they can be remarkably useless for answering the *why*.

And, keeping them Connected and Current ... in line with ever-changing business goals ... is an immense challenge because business goals can change almost literally overnight, while changing metrics and the reporting systems they rely on can be a months-long effort.

Enter analytics.

Analytics agility

In their early years, the information technology analytics relied on were easily as cumbersome and hard to change as metrics reporting systems, and in fact they were often the same system: the enterprise data warehouse.

This arrangement had a significant advantage going for it: It provided a mechanism for exploring the raw data on which metrics were based, giving companies the ability to understand them more deeply.

But data warehouses are hard to design, hard to build, and hard to feed. And once established they're hard to change. They become one more piece of the extensive investments in business infrastructure that make staying the same so much more appealing to business leaders than engaging in the hard work of making change happen.

Enter "big data" – arguably the most misleading name and business case ever applied to an important technology.

When big data first burst into the awareness of corporate America, the stories told about it were all about the growing flood of information available for analysis. Jet engines, for example, generate approximately 20 terabytes of data an hour.[7] Just think of what you could do with all that data, once you have the means to handle it!

Answer: Most of us have no idea. More to the point, most businesses don't own a lot of big-data generators that pump out bytes the way a jet engine does. Many businesses don't even have medium-size data.

But this is a case where size doesn't matter. What does matter: The technology big data management relies on. Without diving deep into the technical details, here's what you need to know about it: It doesn't require extensive up-front design.

Unlike data warehouses, companies can set up big-data repositories pretty quickly and just start dumping data into them. The operative phrase is "schema on demand," where schema refers to how data structures are designed. So unlike a data warehouse, with all of its up-front planning and implementation costs,

---

[7] For the non-mathematically minded reader, 20 terabytes = A LOT.

with big-data technologies analysts can assemble data into whatever analysis they need to perform, when the time comes to perform it.

Analytics expert, Thomas Davenport, writes, "From a technology standpoint, there are a variety of developments coming together: Watson-like cognitive systems for digesting text, big data analytics, rule-based systems, machine learning for developing automated models, and various other branches of artificial intelligence. AI is still best at making narrowly-defined decisions, but it's clearly moving in the direction of broad intelligence. The best systems will combine several or all of these tools; after all, our brains can employ a variety of ways to address a problem." He elaborates on cognitive computing systems, "As with big data or e-commerce, the first thing a management team should do about a new technology is to learn what it is capable of. What are the key elements of cognitive technologies? How might they affect marketing, customer service, and R&D? What kinds of applications exist to support these different business functions? And just how good are the decisions made in these areas?"

Thomas Davenport's Blog: http://www.tomdavenport.com

So the current state of the art for business analytics is that, while there are still plenty of pitfalls, the available technologies and practices are such that they can support businesses with shrinking stay-the-same to change ratios, providing answers to quantitative questions.

Pitfalls? Of course. You can rely on your accounting system specifically because of all the time and effort put into its design and implementation – 500 years, more or less, if you start with when Pacioli first invented the discipline.

With schema-on-demand data analysis there are plenty of ways to inadvertently get the wrong answer to the right question, starting with data quality. Valid statistical analysis depends on data passing several tests. If you're a trained statistician you know all about these tests. If you aren't, consult a trained statistician before engaging in statistical analysis.

Once you've cleared this first hurdle ...

Causes and effects

If you can't model you can't manage. And metrics aren't very useful for modeling, unlike statistical analysis, which is, so long as you know what you're doing.

Analytics are all about spotting patterns in your data, and in particular about spotting correlations.

Example: One of us (Scott Lee) worked with a university that had a clear challenge to overcome: About 40 percent of its stu-students dropped out before the Office of Student Retention had a chance to intervene, half of them in their first year.

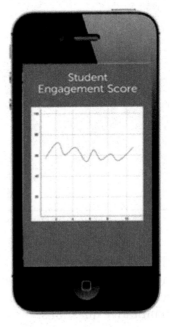

The university had implemented so-called "best practices" from one of the top student administration packages in the industry. In this case, industry best practices revolved around student performance metrics. And yet the information arrived too late, was incomplete and not available to anyone who could affect the outcome. It violated at least half of the 6Cs – not fully Connected, not Complete, and definitely not Current.

The solution required the university to abandon metrics in favor of analytics. Rather than measure performance, the new solution analyzed student engagement patterns to predict their outcomes.

The first step was to collect all of the data that was available from various sensors such as classroom attendance and use of learning tools such as library systems, assignment portals, email, and tutors.

Most of the assets used for learning have some digital signature that indicates that the student is engaged and for how long, which is why we use the term "sensor." The university was able to analyze its student engagement information and compare it to the engagement patterns from similar students who successfully graduated.

The predicted outcome was then transformed into an easy-to-understand visualization on a mobile application on the student's mobile phone. And, the predicted outcome was sent to the Office of Student Retention to trigger early intervention.

The system provides near real-time "tells" – indications of which students no longer exhibit engagement patterns predictive of success, and which, for that matter, exhibit engagement patterns that predict accelerated graduation.

We'd like to tell you the solution was widely accepted across the university, but while the students embraced it, the stay-the-sameness of some of the faculty and administration created pushback.

Sadly, and surprisingly for a group of academics, when it came to student retention this university lacked a culture of honest inquiry – the habit of evidence-based decision-making for running its business, even when the evidence leads to uncomfortable conclusions.

While analytics are, or at least can be the new metrics, there are, of course, challenges.

For example: Compared to metrics, which tend to be constructed in the form of simple ratios, analytics depend on statistical techniques like multiple regression analysis, analysis of variance, Box-Jenkins analysis, and multidimensional scaling. Even knowing which of these techniques to use requires a significant level of expertise; knowing how to use them properly requires more.

And when you're done, what you have is some form of correlation. And as we all know, correlation doesn't prove causation.

Except that in the world of business it usually does.

Not really, but it often does imply it. When the subject is epidemiology, proving causation affects mortality. In the world of business, in contrast, a strong correlation combined with a measure of good sense is usually more than good enough, and far better than doing nothing different than before.

Or, as in the case of the university, it sometimes makes sense to not worry about what the cause and the effect is. Often, all you need to know is that a pattern can successfully predict an outcome. Which leads to one final modification of Drucker's Metrics Dictum: "If you can predict, you can manage."

5. Judgment Day

Judgment Day

"Knowledge is knowing that a tomato is a fruit, wisdom is not putting it in a fruit salad." - Miles Kington

Metrics provide information. Analytics provide knowledge. Great decisions require judgment.

This is, by the way, neither more nor less true for cognitive enterprises than for industrial ones, except for these three differences: (1) Because of the shrinking stay-the-same/change ratio that's leading companies to be more cognitive, important decisions are required more frequently than in the industrial age of business; (2) for so many reasons, more of your workforce at more levels of the organization will be in a position to make important decisions; and (3) increasingly, "important decisions" will be about winning, about beating competitors, rather than being about cutting costs and improving internal efficiencies.

You might as well make sure the whole organization is good at making important decisions, then.

Once upon a time, the best decisions came from nothing but judgment and experience applied to a few standard printed reports, because that's all that was available for business decision-makers to use. When a mainframe computer that cost millions of dollars was equipped with maybe 64K of RAM (only it wasn't RAM, it was something much slower) and the storage medium of choice was tape, notions like big-data analytics were barely mentioned, even in science fiction.

So once business executives needed more than just the plain unvarnished analysis available in hand-coded computerized reports, their judgment and experience were pretty much it.

All they could do was to trust their guts.

Sadly, that is how a large number of business executives, encouraged by a horde of anti-cognition enablers,[8] make important decisions today.

Does this make any sense?

Thinking 101

A premise: People who understand a situation make better decisions than those who don't, all other things being equal.

Assuming you're willing to assume that premise, here's a model for you: Making the best decisions about the most important subjects requires wisdom, which depends on good judgment, which in its turn requires knowledge, built on information, which is obtained by analyzing data.

Figure 5-1 shows these as increasing levels of cognitive abstraction, and value when it comes to decision-making – as an as-

---

[8] Yes, we are talking about Malcolm Gladwell's *Blink: The Power of Thinking Without Thinking* (2007), especially as two-thirds of the book pointed out how much more often *Blink*ing doesn't work.

cending pyramid.

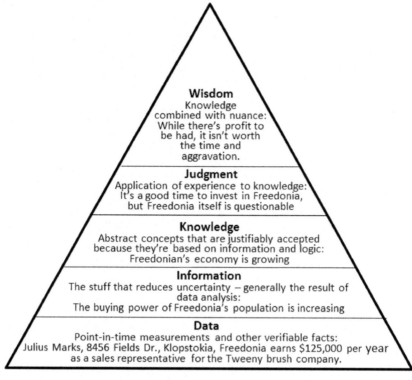

Wisdom
Knowledge combined with nuance: While there's profit to be had, it isn't worth the time and aggravation.

Judgment
Application of experience to knowledge: It's a good time to invest in Freedonia, but Freedonia itself is questionable

Knowledge
Abstract concepts that are justifiably accepted because they're based on information and logic: Freedonian's economy is growing

Information
The stuff that reduces uncertainty – generally the result of data analysis: The buying power of Freedonia's population is increasing

Data
Point-in-time measurements and other verifiable facts: Julius Marks, 8456 Fields Dr., Klopstokia, Freedonia earns $125,000 per year as a sales representative for the Tweeny brush company.

Figure 5- 1. Levels of cognition

Data = Verifiable Facts

Data is the pyramid's foundation. Everything rests on it, or, to use a phrase from the ancient days of computing, GIGO (garbage in, garbage out).

Just to make sure we're talking about the same thing, when we refer to *data* (or, collectively, *evidence*) we'll be talking about facts, verifiable elements of or attributes about something.

For this simple illustration, the home address and annual earnings of an individual who lives in Freedonia are facts – chunks of data.

When you read about the information explosion, those whose words you're reading are probably talking about the explosion of data. And then, not entirely, because it's only data when it is in principle, verifiable. Even then it's only data to the extent you trust its source. So when the pilot announces on the intercom that you're flying at 35,000 feet and the outside temperature is 40 degrees, it's data because you could, in principle, read the appropriate dials, and take the instruments back to a controlled environment to verify their calibration.

But really, it's data because most of us trust pilots not to lie about such things, because why would they?

It isn't, by the way, actual data that Julius Marks lives in Freedonia and makes $125,000. We made that up, and as Freedonia is a country invented by the Marx Brothers we're pretty sure there is no such address. But it is data in the sense we stated it as a fact and it can, in principle, be verified were you to care enough to do so.

One more point about data before moving on: Even if every bit of data at your disposal is accurate, that doesn't mean your data are accurate.

Imagine you rely on a particular source of news. When that source of news runs stories about Freedonians, it always chooses accompanying photos of exceptionally attractive members of that society; just as when it reports on happenings in Sylvania the photos it chooses unfailingly include people of very limited visual appeal.

Every story this imaginary source runs passes a fact check, and the photos are of real people who do live in those countries.

And yet, the conclusions you'll draw regarding the relative attractiveness of the denizens of these two great nations would be completely wrong.

This is a potential pitfall when your use of data is informal. It's an even bigger potential pitfall when your plan for data is to use it in statistical analysis.

Statisticians apply stringent rules with respect to data quality. Some of the rules are arcane, known only to professional statisticians and statistician-like researchers who have to know these things. Others are as basic as the sample bias of our imaginary example.

Our advice: Before you rely on any analysis of your data,

have a professional statistician have a look at it first.

It's that GIGO thing, rearing its ugly head.

A few words about experience

Experience, someone once explained, is just-too-late learning. That's all too accurate, but it masks two other critically important aspects of experience, one positive, the other negative.

The positive: Your experience is the most verifiable data you have. It happened to you, and even allowing for the fallibilities of memory, it's still more reliable than any other data you might have at your disposal.

It's also less reliable than a lot of it, for a subtle but simple reason: Your experience is a biased sample, just as much as our Freedonians vs Sylvanians example. It isn't reliably representative of the world as a whole because few of us set out to live our lives so as to obtain a random sample of all the possible experiences collective humanity might have.

Value your experience for its genuineness. When your experience lines up reasonably well with a situation you're facing, take advantage of it without qualms as it probably is a reasonable sample for whatever sort of situation you're facing.

But don't ever try to persuade yourself that your experience paints you an unbiased picture of the world as it is.

Information = being less uncertain

By itself, data does nothing for you. Information does.

According to the standard Data, Information, Knowledge, Wisdom (DIKW) model we used as our starting point, information is data that's been processed for usefulness. But that just explains where information comes from, not what it is.

Fortunately, an exact definition of *information* has been available since 1963, when Shannon and Weiner first proposed it.[9] Shorn of its mathematical formulae, information is the stuff that reduces uncertainty. It's measured in bits, one bit being the information you need to resolve your uncertainty as to which way

---

[9] In book form: *The Mathematical Theory of Communication*, Claude E. Shannon and Warren Weaver, 1971.

a tossed coin landed, or to cut your uncertainty in half about the result of two coin tosses.

There's rarely any point in trying to quantify the information content of the various sources that cross your desk. There's very much a point to asking which ones reduce your uncertainty about something that matters to you.

You might imagine you run a Freedonian financial services company. In your databases you have annual incomes and various other pieces of data about your clients. If you assume you have enough data that you can adjust for sample biases and such, you could use your databases to estimate the collective annual income of all of Freedonia's citizens. This is a number that greatly reduces your uncertainty about something that matters to you a great deal – how much Freedonia's citizens have to spend on *stuff* every year, including the financial products and services your firm has to offer.

Or, you could look up the information in the *CIA World Factbook*, which includes extensive *information* about Freedonia – information developed from data collected from a vast array of sources and processed to answer questions about every country on earth, including Freedonia. This information is categorized by demography, geography and the economy – useful information for an organization wanting to do business in Freedonia.

But a caution here. Information reduces your uncertainty, but, with trivial exceptions, it can't eliminate it.

Some of your remaining uncertainty might be due to insufficient granularity. For example, the *CIA World Factbook* might not break down the information you're looking for to individual cities, towns and villages. So when you need information about, say, Klopstokia, you'll have to estimate it based on the information you do have. Estimation means residual uncertainty.

Sometimes, your residual uncertainty comes from not being sure you can trust your source. Can you rely on the *CIA World Factbook* to publish undistorted analyses? Can you trust both its authors' motives and their competence?

It's a nice irony that while information is the stuff that's supposed to reduce your uncertainty, you'll never be entirely free of uncertainty regarding the quality of the information itself – something that's even true if you're an eyewitness to events, which anyone knows who has ever watched a stage magician at work.

Information is useful in making a certain class of decision, namely, fairly mundane and mechanical decisions that separate alternatives, one of which is chosen based on a specific type of information that's readily available.

If, for example, you're a retailer and you need to know how much of a specific SKU you have to ship to your store in, say, Klopstokia from your distribution center in Marseilles, you can use information from your inventory database, combined with demand forecasts provided by the merchant responsible for the relevant product line to decide.

You can. That doesn't mean you should. Knowledge, the next level of abstraction, has a role to play as well.

Knowledge = putting your uncertainty behind you

While two mathematicians were able to give us a precise definition of information, it took Plato to define *knowledge* and a philosopher of science, Karl Popper, to give us a proper understanding of it.

Plato first: He taught that knowledge requires three conditions: You have to believe something is true, you have to have a good reason for believing it's true, and it has to actually be true.

It's one of those definitions that's clear but useless, because it depends on someone, somewhere, having some way of knowing what's actually true. Otherwise there's no way to meet the third condition for sure: Unless someone, somewhere, has access to the "truth" somehow, even the great guru on the mountain has nothing more to go on than believing something to be true and having a good reason for believing it.

Enter Karl Popper. Popper studied science as it really happens, and discovered something remarkable: Scientists never prove anything. Never. If a scientist is ever certain of anything, that scientist isn't practicing science at the time.

Far from trying to prove something, what scientists are always trying to do is to disprove something, generally something they can't directly observe. What they'll do is reason: "If the earth is flat, then if I watch a ship sail away into the distance, it should get smaller and smaller until it's too small to see, or else suddenly vanish as it falls off the edge."

They then perform the experiment or go out into nature, and observe. In this case they use a telescope to watch ships as they sail away into the distance. Were they to see the ships getting steadily smaller they wouldn't have proven the world is flat. Other theories might predict the same thing, like maybe light bends to follow the earth's surface no matter what its shape, or perhaps the ships got wet, were subjected to a hot wind, and like a cotton shirt, really did shrink.

But in fact, what the scientists saw while watching ships sail away was the ships disappearing from the bottom up. Voila! They've successfully disproven the theory that the earth is flat. Doesn't this mean they've proven the earth is round? Nope. Exercise for the reader: Develop two theories that would also account for how ships vanish that don't depend on the earth being round.

When scientists say they "know" something, it's a shorthand for saying they and their colleagues have tried really, really hard to disprove it, with all the ingenuity at their disposal, and thus far they've failed. So until someone else comes up with an even more ingenious test, the theory in question is the best explanation they have.

Apply this to the world of business. You have a theory that workforce morale is poor. You ask yourself: If morale is poor, what would you be likely to find out in the wilds of the cubical farm?

You answer yourself: "Self," you say, "you should see employees with sullen expressions, shuffling along without much energy, except when you see displays of anger."

So you walk to their natural habitat, a conference room, but before you go inside you hear raised voices and angry shouting.

Satisfied, you walk away, sure you've proven morale is bad.

But you'd be completely wrong. What you'd actually accomplished was that you'd failed to disprove your theory that morale is bad.

A different test would have disproved your theory. In this case it would have been to listen to the words being spoken. Because what was really going on was that your business is located in Wisconsin, this is a Monday, and yesterday the Packers blew a big lead and lost an easy one.

You never know anything in the absolute sense. "Knowing" something means being confident your theory about something won't be disproven in the future, not that you have access to "the truth."

Because you don't. When people say they're telling the truth they're doing no such thing. We humans don't have access to "the truth." When people say they're telling the truth what they mean is they're being completely honest – not something to be taken lightly, but not the same thing.

Knowledge is higher on the pyramid than information, and narrower, because while you might have lots and lots of information about lots and lots of subjects, if you're honest with yourself you'll acknowledge that the number of subjects about which you're confident enough of your opinion to say you know what's going on is quite a lot smaller than the number about which you have information at your disposal.

Judgment = knowledge + experience, applied

You're watching a stage magician. The information at hand tells you a young woman is floating in mid-air.

Do you conclude the magician used psychokinetic powers to negate the pull of gravity? If so, can we interest you in investing in our space elevator company?

When a magician levitates someone on stage, you don't conclude they have psychokinetic powers. You don't because you have other information and knowledge at your disposal, and quite a lot of experience, that tells you there are other, better explanations for what you're seeing.

You are in a position to apply judgment to the situation.

Business example: Analysis of various data sources might suggest Freedonia's economy has been steadily growing for the past decade. That isn't something you know, but it is information – you're less uncertain about the state of Freedonia's economy than before you started because various economic indicators provide a consistent picture.

You need to decide whether to invest in Freedonia's economy

– a move that enriches you if Freedonia's economy really is grow-ing and if it continues to do so; and that shrinks your personal pit-tance significantly if the Freedonian economy falters.

If information was the end of things, the growth information would tell you to pursue it. But information isn't the end of things when it comes to making important decisions.

You decide to ask a colleague who speaks Freedonian. He "knows" Freedonians are lazy and aren't to be trusted, and tells you as much. Because he "knows" this he isn't about to endorse a Freedonian investment strategy.

Based on your colleague's tone of voice and choice of words you infer his opinion of Freedonians is a matter of personal bias, not reliable data. And so, you decide to ignore an opinion.

That is, you apply your judgment.

You also consult other colleagues – ones whose qualifications go beyond speaking the language to having actually conducted business in Freedonia. They all tell you the Freedonian govern-ment imposes so much bureaucracy on businesses that it ham-strings their ability to export products that would otherwise be quite competitive.

Their collective knowledge is, for you, useful information. Add to that your own knowledge and experience, which tell you government bureaucracy rarely diminishes over time, and that an economy, burdened with a private sector hamstrung by excessive paperwork, is unlikely to thrive in the long run.

Your *judgment* tells you to avoid Freedonian investments as a bad long-term play.

Wisdom

Getting tired of the pyramid? Us too. We'll sum up quickly:

Wisdom is judgment expanded to give us timeless, subtle, nuanced principles we can rely on, along with an understanding that principles have their limits. Every situation is just different enough that the principle we want to apply might or might not fit the situation well enough to provide appropriate guidance.

Wisdom is judgment tempered by humility.

If you're looking for wisdom in business you can stop look-ing. For the most part, business isn't where wisdom resides.

The point of this section

No question about it – the preceding was abstract and possibly quite tedious. It came dangerously close to epistemology, among the most eye-glazing of philosophical disciplines.

We make no apology because when it comes to the cognitive enterprise there's nothing more important than understanding cognition, especially as it applies to making great decisions.

Decisions

First, an observation: In business, it isn't a decision unless it commits or denies time, staff and budget. Unless it results in action. Everything else is just talking about it.

Second, a hard-to-track-down statistic: Someone analyzed mortality under a range of historical generals. The result: The troops who fought for generals who most often made great decisions were the most likely to survive. Those who fought for generals who habitually made any decision at all were the second-most likely to survive.

Troops who fought for generals who dithered were the ones who were most often slaughtered where they stood.

Third: Observe, orient, decide, act, rinse and repeat: It's what's called the OODA loop.

OODA

In military doctrine, maneuver warfare holds the current key to success. It works through a process-like formula called the OODA loop (observation, orientation, decision, and action) developed by Colonel John Boyd after the Vietnam War debacle.

According to OODA theory, whichever side has the faster OODA loops generally wins, because from the perspective of their opponent, faster loops makes their actions unpredictable, while from their own perspective their opponent's decisions no longer matter – by the time they're turned into action it's too late to turn them into action.

Which doesn't, however, mean decision-making has been reduced to a predictable, repeatable process. Far from it. Speeding up your OODA loops only works when the accuracy of observation and orientation, the suitability of decisions, and the level of skill applied to actions taken don't suffer.

If this weren't the case, any decision made quickly enough would win, as would action no matter how sloppily executed. But that isn't the case.

For while indecision almost always leads to failure, the world has no shortage of stupid losers whose only ability is to make snap decisions without first understanding the situation.

And while failing to act guarantees losing even more than failing to decide, taking action certainly doesn't guarantee winning. It's the ability to execute that in the end makes the difference.

To the extent business tactics resemble military tactics,[10] OODA theory can help businesses beat competitors just as it helps military leaders beat opposing forces.

OODA has an interesting property when compared to other business popular loops like PDCA (plan, do, check, act). PDCA and similar loops all have an *inward* focus. They're about making the organization more efficient and effective. OODA, in contrast, while it requires an effective organization (the Act part of the loop), has an *external* focus.

PDCA is about being better at something. OODA is about winning. Which is why OODA loops emphasize speed, while PDCA loops don't.

Perhaps they should: shrinking stay-the-same/change ratios mean the faster an organization gets better, the better.

More to the point for a cognitive enterprise is that OODA theory demands decision-making that's both fast and accurate. Fast, accurate decision-making doesn't require more information and faster ways of processing data to get it. It requires fast access to and creation of knowledge and judgment in forms that can be applied to business decisions.

Which leads to this: Cognitive enterprises have more knowledge at their disposal than the other kinds. Not more knowledge. More knowledge at their disposal.

---

[10] Less than you might think, but enough.

OODA and Cognition

Take one more look at the OODA loop and you'll see: It's a pretty good model for thinking. You observe – you notice something interesting that gives you something to think about. You orient – you think about it, applying what you know about similar-seeming phenomena and also what you know about the limitations of your knowledge and experience. You decide – assuming what you noticed calls for you to do something about it, you assess the alternatives available to you and choose the one that seems best. And you act – you carry out your decision.

Then you observe what happened and start over. Sure looks like thinking to us, whether it's done by a human being or by an enterprise.

What a cognitive enterprise knows

In our consulting careers there has been only one constant: No matter what the challenge, the expertise needed to deal with the situation has always been there, in the heads of the company's employees, just waiting to be shared with the company's decision-makers.

Good business leaders are smart enough to take advantage of that knowledge without any consulting help.

They'll take advantage of it in two ways. The first is to create listening channels where employees can share what they know about a subject when leaders need that knowledge.

The second is to not need that knowledge, by giving employees the authority to make as many decisions as possible. Among the advantages: Acting on knowledge is both faster and cheaper than explaining that knowledge well enough for someone else to act on it.

It's OODA squared. First, each decision has a shorter cycle time because there's no need to explain things. And second, the company has more decision-makers, which means decisions don't sit in a queue waiting to be made by busy executives who are now the primary bottleneck to OODA-loop speeds.

Leaders of cognitive enterprises will go way beyond this. As pointed out in another chapter, all enterprises are, like it or not, becoming more permeable. In addition to the knowledge available within the enterprise, the social web means much more knowledge is available within the ecosystem – the communities, enabled by the social web, that penetrate the enterprise without being part of it – free for the asking.

But the best business leaders, of the most cognitive enterprises, will find ways to take these thoughts even further. They'll recognize the difference between someone in the enterprise knowing something and the enterprise knowing it.

The enterprise knows something when most of its workforce understands it and has no residual doubts about it.

The more the enterprise knows, the more cognitive it is.

Metrics provide information. Analytics provide knowledge.

Leveraging the ecosystem is one way the social web can provide competitively useful knowledge. There's a second way that's potentially transformational.

The key is the difference between metrics and analytics: Metrics provide information while analytics provide knowledge. Not *certainty*, nothing can provide that; but reliable enough, competitively invaluable patterns that decision-makers can use with confidence.

This is what business decision-makers need – *knowledge*. Not data or information. Competitive knowledge. Insights about customers, communities, their own capabilities and those of competitors that they can use to make faster and better business decisions and then act on them effectively.

Every year, business stakeholders tell IT to get them more knowledge. They pony-up the money and every time IT falls short of their expectations.

Why?

In part it's a failure of vocabulary – a failure to understand the clear but subtle distinctions of the DIKJW pyramid. Because while most business decision-makers want knowledge and think they're asking for it, the word they use is information and they ask for the ability to work with it.

The ongoing business obsession with metrics doesn't help, either.

Meanwhile, IT executives, managers and on-the-ground professionals are inundated with the advice of a punditocracy that often resembles nothing so much as a bunch of parrots all parroting each other. Only one or two ever did know what the flock they were talking about, and it doesn't take long for their original message, even if it was insightful, to get lost through imperfect and repeated repetition.

Which in this case means IT thinks their "internal customers" want more and more tools so they can "analyze big data to turn it into information."

Where does the big data come from? It must come from the company's databases and the transactions that feed them.

All of IT's controls, governance models, and solution-design habits are designed for data and information owned by the organization. Transactional data, master data, metadata, the stuff IT processes and takes care of, that's what their "internal customers" must be looking for.

Isn't it? IT sure hopes so, because that's what it's good at.

Uh … no.

Profiling

Right now, many of your customers, employees, suppliers, business partners, students or whoever you think is valuable to your organization are generating four new dimensions of personal data. They're leaving breadcrumbs and trails that let businesses that value knowledge about their customers build insightful *engagement*, *psychographic*, *physiological*, and *consumption* profiles. With the right analytical care, and adherence to the Don't Be Creepy Rule (sidebar) they can provide profitable guidance on how your company should engage with each of these individuals to its advantage, while revealing patterns that can help you predict how similar individuals will respond to your company as it develops new products, marketing campaigns, and approaches to managing customer relationships.

You won't find engagement, psychographic, physiological and consumption cues in your business systems. They're out there in the social web. They aren't in your business systems but you'll need to link them to your business systems.

ETGers in particular are leaving whole loaves of these bread-crumbs behind for anyone to find and use, but not only ETGers are leaving useful breadcrumbs. Anyone who has an online life leaves some of them behind.

Engagement profiling

Engagement profiling is a matter of gaining insights into customers and other members of your business ecosystem by becoming more aware of which web sites they visit and subscribe to, especially social web sites, but certainly not limited to them.

The Don't Be Creepy Rule

As you develop profiles, you'll gain insights about your customers, your employees, and other members of your business ecosystem, they might not even have about themselves.

Apply these insights too overtly and you'll be creepy.

Don't do this.

By all means, use your insights to more intelligently plan how you engage.

But don't parade your knowledge. In marketing copy this is the difference between, "As someone who suffers from eczema, you'll want to know about our new ointment ..." and "Do you suffer from eczema? If so, you might want to know about a new product we're offering."

All it takes is a bit of empathy and a dash of good judgment to stay on the right side of the line that separates helpfulness from creepiness.

Even in its most elementary form an engagement profile can prove valuable. It is, for example, a pretty good bet that someone who has registered with Dogster will be more receptive to a dog food sales pitch than a sales target you know nothing about.

By considering website visits as *tells* you can develop a more sophisticated engagement profile just as another poker player's tells give you information about the cards he's holding.

You can, for example, draw inferences about important life events from the websites a customer visits and subscribes to:

someone who signs up for real estate listing services, reviews neighborhood crime statistics, and runs the numbers with various online mortgage services is getting ready to move into a new residence. This is obvious to a human being who decides to look at an individual, that is. The challenge is getting it to scale.

Psychographic profiles

Psychographic profiles help you understand someone's personality and state of mind – information that's of obvious value when you're constructing a sales argument, but is of even more value when you're trying to make the best hire possible for an open position.

You can find the data you need to construct psychographic profiles across the social web. Obvious places such as Facebook, Twitter and LinkedIn. And not so obvious places such as Craigslist, blogs, news, forums and variety of specialized venues.

Even more than when constructing an engagement profile, humans, accustomed to reading what someone writes and drawing inferences about their personality and state of mind, have an easier time of it than computers. Because where an engagement profile depends on interpreting where someone goes on the Web, their psychographic profile depends on what they write.

This is a rapidly developing area. Two tips: (1) use the engagement profile to discover life events; and then, (2) based on what life event is impending, look for suggestive phrases in what someone posts online.

For example, if someone who is buying a house (life event) includes in a Facebook post the words "bigger house," you can infer a very different frame of mind, economic situation, and stage of life than someone else who is also buying a house but uses the word "downsizing."

Participants in the digital communities that comprise the social web willingly let their guard down to speak with anyone who will hear what they have to say on any subject. They tell their fellow community members what they like, dislike, want, and need, their lifestyle preferences, when and where they are going and who their friends and family are.

Are they naïve? Perhaps. Exhibitionistic? Maybe. Possibly

they've simply drawn a different boundary between what they consider public and private. It also could be that with more than 7 billion people on this planet they're doing what they can to be more than just an extra in someone else's movie.

From the perspective of the cognitive enterprise, their motivation for sharing so much of themselves online doesn't matter very much. What does matter is that they do, which is why social networks have become the new marketing frontier with literally endless personal data attributes created directly by their subscribers. Certainly the ETGers are there in large numbers, but if you think it's only the ETG, take a look at TripAdvisor's destination and hotel reviews. Look at Amazon's product reviews. Look at ... heck, it really doesn't matter what you look at. You'll find that in the aggregate, millions of people express their opinions about thousands of subjects, all over the social web.

As they do they make the same information available to potential marketers. Those who understand the social interaction and the content within a social network can use this information to develop a psychologically oriented biography known as a psychographic profile.

Remember that for the cognitive enterprise the formula is Customers, Communities and Capabilities. With the *capability* to construct psychographic profiles comes the ability to understand what *customers* are saying about your company, directly influencing attitudes about your company throughout the *communities* they're members of. And because they're members of these communities they have instant credibility.

By being able to construct psychographic profiles your company can be in a position to intervene before negative attitudes about you spread uncontrollably.

The early adopters of social media were largely in the demographic age group of 18-25, the generational ETG. Older generations became apprentice ETGers soon after, with large scale adoption into every demographic category.

Many users now connect to these social networks with a smartphone app that encourages continuous communication among members of the online communities they belong to. So engaged is the population that many ETGers spend more time interacting with their social networks than watching TV, and many more, especially among the ETG, multiplex their time as two-screen consumers of entertainment, enjoying television programming augmented in real time with complementary smartphone or tablet-oriented content. It's why we've seen a shift in advertising dollars to the social web. Even non-cognitive enterprises know they need to be where their customers are.

Kinetic profiles

The popularity of smartphones and tablets has spawned more creativity in the emerging market of wearable technology. Fitness vendors have developed wearable wristbands that track exercise activity, sleep patterns and food consumption. Not to be outdone, smartphone designers like Apple and Samsung are including similar capabilities in their smartwatches.

More precise and targeted medical devices are also emerging that have similar form factors and monitor vital signs, blood sugar and oxygen, pain, and medication consumption – emerging support for telemedicine.

The importance of these devices to the cognitive enterprise is significant in proportion to the value of understanding an individual's health and correlating it with engagement, psychology, and consumption.

It's worth noting that along the way, the unregulated and exchange-shared fitness data collected by wearable fitness monitors and smart watch apps are likely to start blurring the currently well-defined boundary that walls off PII (personally identifiable information) and PHI (personal health information) among participants in the healthcare industry.

It isn't just health and fitness data, either. For example, some insurance companies are already using wearable or kinetic technologies to offer discounts to companies that share their fleet driving data, using specialized GPS systems that compare driving speeds to the local speed limit. The smart insurers offer safe driving discounts. Those whose marketing departments are run by actuaries who establish risk-based rate penalties.

It's far from unimaginable that future health insurers will offer premium discounts for healthy lifestyles, tracked by specialized GPS systems that know when an insured enters an exercise facility and when a different insured walks into a Dunkin' Donuts.

As the ability to track customer and employee location and behaviors increases, the ability of the cognitive enterprise to interpret this information increases as well.

As does the importance of the Don't Be Creepy Rule as your company rushes to take advantage of the opportunity before faster-moving competitors do.

Consumption profile

Untethered networks are enabling remote control of consumer products. These "smart products" (products whose functionality is controlled by microprocessors coupled with built-in connectivity) are integrated into the so-called IoT (Internet of Things).

While remote control is what provides the obvious customer benefit that will drive adoption of smart products, their value to the cognitive enterprise owes more to the massive amounts of data they can generate – in all likelihood, more than all other sources combined. With smart products you will be able to remotely:

- Change the thermostat in your weekend cabin so it's warm when you arrive.
- See who's ringing your doorbell while you're on vacation, and speak with them.
- Start pre-heating the oven.
- Reprogram your DVR.
- Find your ETG offspring now that curfew has passed. Assuming, of course, your ETG offspring hasn't figured out how to gimmick the system.
- And whatever else ingenious inventors will come up with will motivate an increasing number of consumers, as always led by the ETG but quickly followed by the merely technically literate, to connect everything they own to the social web.

It isn't only remote control, either. Automobiles are now connected to provide roadside assistance, maintenance reminders ... and even better, early warnings of impending maintenance problems ... along with turn-by-turn directions. Televisions are connected to the Internet to deliver content from entertainment providers such as Netflix and Hulu.

This rapidly expanding array of connected, largely autonomous devices will make it possible for cognitive enterprises to create a profile of the devices' operations and usages, and by inference their customers' consumption behavior, to any marketer with a large enough budget to buy the information. Current estimates from Cisco, among others, say there will hundreds of billions of devices in the foreseeable future.

In addition, product managers will have direct, reliable data to use to recognize and address their products' design and manufacturing weaknesses as revealed by product breakdowns during actual use.

A quick how-to

So voluminous is the activity in the social web that exchanges have been established to sell the data for various marketing purposes.

If you were a private detective you could apply your knowledge and judgment to the trail of breadcrumbs an individual you're investigating has left behind.

But you aren't a private investigator. You're part of a cognitive enterprise, which means you need to be able to do what a private investigator might do, only at scale.

Contemporary social web applications, and for that matter, not-so-contemporary meat-and-potatoes services like banking, require a unique identifier that's connected to their subscribers' digital lives. The most common is a personal email address, because (1) it's unique, unless and until the subscriber's email password is hacked; and (2) the organization hosting a given social website can use it to deliver information that doesn't belong on the website itself.

ETGers have more of these subscriptions, but even stodgy codgers buy products online, look for employment opportunities and apply for them; post product reviews; check their bank accounts; and electronically file their taxes. They use their personal email address as their unique identifier for every one of these activities and a dozen others besides. The use of the personal email address is so pervasive that it's the linchpin of a whole persona canny analysts can use to draw engagement inferences regarding an individual's digital life.

Take the example of an ETGer applying for a position on a recruiting web site. Inevitably, in addition to their resume and demographic data, they'll provide their personal email address to be used to identify their information, and to be used for communications.

Recruiting web sites provide electronic data exchange mechanisms to larger employers so they can electronically conduct business without human intervention. Employers access them by means of "application programming interfaces" (APIs) which are open to subscribers. The API mechanism underpins the digital business landscape; which means that wherever people use their personal email addresses to conduct business and haven't accepted the trade-offs associated with insisting on absolute data privacy, there is an API that can be queried to examine their behavior.

A personal email address is the key to tracking an engagement pattern of behavior that can be used in a profiling process by experts in digital forensics or machines programmed to mimic them.

These experts in digital forensics are called data scientists.[11] Something they need to do is connect customer and employee records from internal databases to the engagement, psychographic, kinetic, and consumption profiles they're able to develop from the social web.

But internal IT systems have their own unique identifiers for customer and employee records – an internally assigned key value that has no more meaning in the social web than personal email addresses do in the company's internal databases, probably less. As discussed in the chapter on Information Technology, smart IT organizations are figuring out how to link these two sources of information. If your IT organization isn't actively headed in this direction, what are they, and you, waiting for? You cer-

---

[11] Before the advent of big-data analytics they went by the title "statistician" and commanded significantly lower salaries.

tainly have competitors who already have this capability.

The future of your organization depends on your following suit.

Is it real?

Relatively few organizations take advantage of this potential flood of competitive knowledge.

Why?

As consultants we hear about all the barriers. Security. Privacy. Cost. Consistency.

Second-most-important: The IT priority queue is already full, and we can't afford to push out any of the project backlog any further.

Most important: "Who's done this before?"

If you want your company to be an innovator, you should sincerely hope the answer is, no one. But in this case that isn't the answer. The answer is: Google. Apple. Amazon. Dell.

Something these four innovators have in common is that they haven't forgotten that their job is to out-do competitors. Something else they have in common is that the top executives in all four companies are technically literate – very literate.

One more similarity: Each has invested millions of dollars to embed customer data attributes in their business processes.

Google

Google builds knowledge graphs from 60 trillion web pages using content tagging, collection, and curation processes, then tracks the usage patterns of those who consume it. Few organizations have more real-time data about you than Google.

Apple

Apple's devices are the interfaces to its massive content libraries. Every device is integrated with an Apple account which is tied to a personal email address and virtual wallet. Every activity is monitored to personalize the user experience.

And Apple manages to do all this without violating the Don't Be Creepy Rule: Its customers don't worry about how much Apple knows about them – they appreciate the added convenience that results from it.

Like Google, Apple knows every piece of content consumed on its devices in a real-time feedback loop. Google, which owns Android and has an even larger smartphone installed base than Apple, has adopted the same model.

Amazon

Amazon tracks content consumption in much the same way its customers traverse its digital properties looking for items to purchase or content to consume. It's adopted a multi-surface strategy, which is to say Amazon considers desktop, tablet, mobile, and TV visitors are equal-opportunity buyers.

And Amazon is legendary for being able to use its knowledge of its customers to suggest other products and services they might be interested in.

Do you see a pattern here?

Dell

Google, Apple and Amazon collect, turn into knowledge, and use data their customers generate themselves.

Dell does the same and adds social profile data. By listening and collecting social data, Dell can add significant psychographic details to its business and consumer customer profiles.

These innovators combine three very important customer data points by correlating what they see, what they say and what they've done in the past to predict outcomes.

You've experienced some of this firsthand and undoubtedly recognized it while it was happening. Other experiences are more subliminal.

Google autocomplete provides personalized search results as you type your search criteria. Amazon and Apple make recommendations as soon as you search for products or content on their digital venues. Dell is more subtle, using predictive algorithms in its business-to-business sales to prioritize opportunities based on size, profitability, and likelihood of success.

While the details for all three companies are proprietary,

they all follow a distinct pattern of using consumer-generated data to establish priority, timeline, context and identity in support of more cognitive engagement patterns.

What makes these companies and their kindred cognitive enterprises special? They don't plod, and they despise ignorance. They actively look for opportunities to collect every piece of data customers and potential customers generate about themselves, use it to identify and fulfill their needs, and don't waste months or years agonizing about the investment.

Is it real for you?

So what about your organization?

By now, few companies lack strategies for consuming "big data," not because they know what they're going to do with it, but, in our experience at least, in order to avoid embarrassment, as the entire business punditocracy has by now established big data analytics as a *sin qua non* of companies that want to survive to the next decade.

Every company is using words like volume, variety, velocity and variability. Technologies like Hadoop, HANA, AWS, and NoSQL, with varying degrees of sophistication about what it will take to implement them, but little clarity regarding the business value they'll provide.

Not so long ago, we were discussing employee retention with a healthcare organization plagued by the uncertainties of new regulations impacting its industry.

Talent was a critical success factor in the organization's business model, as it is in yours and every current and would-be cognitive enterprise. It shared its metrics from its human capital management and patient care systems. We suggested the software it deployed to manage its employees and record their work was fundamentally flawed because it is designed to track repeatable processes.

Why? Healthcare is about relationships. The more time bedside nurses spend tracking and documenting tasks, the less time they spend taking care of patients. Medically, when nurses form personal relationships with patients, thereby helping patients develop a positive attitude, they're doing far more for the medical outcome than when they fill out process-management forms.

And with social media, patients' relationships with their nurses doesn't end when they walk out the hospital door. Patients and nurses "friend" each other in social networks. They share pictures, status updates and ask for and give advice.

Healthcare has become far more than a collection of processes. It's become a community of its own that transcends the legal and physical boundaries of the healthcare provider.

So using traditional process tracking software to manage experts like nurses in the customer experience is not a good thing. These systems have no functionality to measure a patient care provider's most important contributions.

And if, when needing care for some other condition, a patient returns in the future, it will likely be because of the relationships they formed with the staff, or other patients' recommendations read in the social web, and not the organizations' ability to track employee-level task performance in the healthcare process.

To patients and their healthcare providers, to customers and employees in general, everything is personal. You need to keep this in mind as you develop your strategies for gaining knowledge about your customers and employees.

The steps

So how do you engage the ETG, on their terms?

Get permission. In every engagement opportunity, you must solicit their permission to collect information from mobile, social, wearable and IoT. Request permission and have them authenticate with the identity they use in the social web, not the customer or employee number in your business systems.

Secure their data. Take the utmost measures to secure the information from those who want to steal it. Remember, it's a digital world and there are criminals who actively seek out opportunities to cash-in on your incompetence.

Curate the data. Collecting it isn't enough. You need systems to discard what's too unreliable. Your data scientists have to document its limitations, and your systems have to extract useful information from it.

You need technologies that can analyze what people say,

what they see, what they've done in the past, and what they're doing right now.

You need systems that can anchor this information to your business systems.

Then you're ready for the analytics that can turn this information into knowledge.

We call this process *curation* because it pulls things together, sifts through them, makes sure the information is collectively reliable, and makes it presentable for use.

Real-world experience

While engaged with an insurance company struggling to reduce its policy administration costs, we developed a new customer engagement model. We called it digital care. Its purpose was to move tech savvy customers, ETGers regardless of their chronological age, into a lower cost, self-service model built on content and social media.

We solicited customers from various touch points such as Web sites, social media and email, asking them to participate in a digital care survey. In exchange they would receive a personalized gift of limited value. The gift would be determined from the personal attributes collected by the survey, matched to a wide range of products from our client's pool of thousands of business partners.

In order to take the survey, customers were required to register with the login credentials from their popular social media account (unsurprisingly, most chose Facebook).

With the customer's permission and identity tokens, the insurance company used advanced analytics to transform social media data into rudimentary psychographic profiles for each participant. The profile dealt with only two cognitive dimensions: (1) product and service desirability; and (2) technological savviness.

The products/services were readily available in social media and could easily be matched to offers in the existing vendor database. The process to determine tech savviness required analysis of several data points with predictions of possible outcomes.

To develop this psychographic profile our process counted the number of social media sites used, conversation volume, interest categories, social followers, social reach, calls to existing help desks, any support request by email or social media, document downloads, and usage of existing self-service content. A statistical model produced a score used to rank stack the population.

The result: The insurance company determined it could move more than 20 percent of its ETG-like customer base into a digital care model with little to no training, while another 15 percent could be successfully trained in its use. The digital care model would be designed to listen for life events and requests for information which would be fulfilled with automated content distribution through social media and mobile apps.

Digital care moved ETGers from telephone, email and mass-content support into a lower-cost mode that provided social and mobile care with very personalized responses. Instead of continuing its decades-long attempts to commoditize policy administration operations, it now reduced its processing costs while personalizing them. And we accomplished this with only one dimension of ETG personal data.

All of this was accomplished in a 4-month project. Imagine what the insurance company will achieve when it has a multidimensional view.

Imagine what your company could achieve if you had this knowledge about your customers.

6. The Cognitive Model

Canary
A joke:
A business decided to build the perfect factory. Which it did.
This perfect factory had just two employees – a person, and a dog.
The person's job was to feed the dog.
The dog's job was to keep the person from touching anything.

As explained in Chapter 1, the industrial model was (and is) PROCESS, technology, *people*, in descending order of importance. That worked well for industrial businesses – businesses whose success depended on their ability to churn out near-identical copies of whatever it was they had to sell.

For cognitive enterprises – businesses that succeed by being knowledgeable in a collective sense – industrial-age process won't get them there. The reasons are spelled out in Chapter 7. For now, rely on this: The industrial model is about how work gets done – not a small thing, but a means to an end.

The new model that's ... not replacing it, but taking precedence over it ... is Customers, Communities, and Capabilities. What follows is a quick introduction. The chapters that follow put meat on these bones.

Customers

Customers don't appear in the process/technology/people formula.

If well-crafted processes are all a business needs to keep the customers it has and attract new ones, this would be okay. And for businesses selling commodity items, well-crafted processes probably are all that's needed, as it's a company's processes that determine such matters as defect rates and the cost of goods sold.

Businesses that don't want to sell commodity items, on the other hand, invest in customer relationships. It's called the cost of sales, and businesses experience pain when customers defect to competitors.

We aren't going to take a lot of time on customers in this book, in spite of their pre-eminent position in the societal model. There's too much literature already available on the subject. Later on in this chapter we'll cover what we see as some important but under-recognized customer trends. Here, we'll focus on something more important: Understanding what a customer is.

In the process/technology/people world, your customer is whoever's inbox receives the contents of your outbox. In the world of people who understand customers best, sales professionals, this definition is worse than worthless. It's wrong.

Instead, try this: *Customers are the entities that make or strongly influence the decision to buy your company's products and services.*

Those who (or that) haven't yet made this decision but might make it in the future are called "prospects."

This is what cognitive enterprises have to understand in depth: Who (or, on occasion, what) makes the buying decision. The more a business knows about its *customers* and *prospects,* the better every decision it makes will be.

To illustrate the point, five brief examples follow: McDonald's during (1) and after (2) the Ronald McDonald era; (3) non-premium media; (4) the American healthcare system; and (5) fashionable clothing.

McDonald's in the Ronald McDonald Era

Imagine yourself, ten or fifteen years ago, going to McDonald's for lunch some fine day. At another table you see a family – a parent or two with pre-teenage kids. On the table you see food, plus some awesomely cheap and throwaway toys.

The question: Who, back then, was McDonald's customer? Who, that is, made the decision to come to McDonald's for lunch?

The answer is, of course, that the children made this decision, influenced by Ronald McDonald and even more influenced by their desire for new toys.

Mom or Dad provided the cash to buy lunch, but so what? It isn't as though they had a choice. They were merely the *wallets* in this interaction. As everyone in the family presumably consumed what they bought, everyone at the table played the role of *con-*

sumer.

But the kids were McDonald's customers. They made the buying decision and McDonald's knew it, which is why Ronald and his buddies featured so prominently in its advertising.

McDonald's in the post-Ronald-McDonald Era

For whatever reason McDonald's executives decided to stop selling to children and instead to sell to teenagers and Millennials – the very same age group we've been calling the ETG. Without debating the wisdom of this decision, it did more than reposition the brand. Where in the Ronald McDonald era customers, consumers and wallets were different (children, the family, and the parents, respectively), in the post-Ronald-McDonald era the company's customers, consumers and wallets are the same person.

This might, in fact, explain why the "I'm Lovin' It" campaign has been such a dismal failure. When the company's front man was a clown, its customers could decide to eat at McDonald's without having to spend any of their own money on the food. That was Mommy and Daddy's job, and neither the buying decision nor the amount spent had all that much to do with the food itself.

The ETGers McDonald's is trying to sell to now have to shell out their own money to buy their meals. That isn't just a harder sell. It's a *different* sell.

Media

We covered some media aspects in the Finance chapter. Newspaper publishers and other sponsored media sell an artifact – the daily newspaper, weekly or monthly magazine, television programs and such – that bears a superficial resemblance to a product.

But it isn't their product, because they don't make a profit from the readers, viewers, or listeners who consume it. These fine folks make a consumption decision, but only a limited buying decision at best.

From the perspective of the media, it's their readers, viewers and listeners who are their product, which they bundle up and sell to the advertisers who are their customers, consumers, and wallets.

U.S. Healthcare

A patient becomes ill and visits a physician. The physician tallies her symptoms, diagnoses the condition that's causing them, and prescribes a treatment, for which the patient's insurance pays most of the cost.

Who is the customer? Who makes the buying decision? The patient, but only when it came to choosing which physician to visit. After that the patient is relegated to the role of consumer. But strangely it's the seller – the physician – who, by prescribing treatments, takes on the role of customer.

Wonderful, isn't it? In the U.S. healthcare system the seller is the customer. No wonder it's such a mess.

As for the insurance company, it's the *wallet*.

Men's fashions

Retailers that sell high-end women's fashions know who their customers are: Affluent women. All of their advertising, store design elements, and sales floor training are geared to address this reality. Depending on the woman she might or might not be the wallet, but she is both the customer and the consumer, no doubt about it.

Retailers that sell high-end men's fashions also know who their customers are, and interestingly enough they're most often the same customer as the one who buys women's fashions.

It isn't the men. They are the consumers who wear the clothing; often they're also the wallet. But in round numbers, 60% or more of these buying decisions are made by the men's wives or other form of female companion ... affluent women. For men's fashion retailers there's no question who the customer is, and that's who they sell to.

And ...

As if it needs to be said, cognitive enterprises want as much knowledge as possible about their customers. It's that knowledge that lets them focus every decision they make on how it will affect their ability to sell more products to more customers.

Not every organization has customers ... nor should they

The model starts with customers, but like all models, it has limitations.

Knowing who your customers are is one of those concepts that's wonderfully useful in the right context, like, when you're running a business and need to understand who you're creating value for and how to persuade them to pay for that value.

And it's worse than useless in the wrong context.

For instance, start with your interpersonal relationships. Do you consider your friends to be your customers? Your spouse? Children? No, of course not. The world of interpersonal relationships is far richer than this.

Institutions of higher learning might do well to stop thinking in provider/customer terms, too. Vendors try to make customers happy. Professors should not be trying to make college students happy. They should be trying to educate them, a condition whose correlation to happiness is uncertain at best.

Many citizens consider themselves to be government's customers. They pay taxes and expect to get value from them. It's a bad model.

We were better off when citizens, in John F. Kennedy's words, asked not what their country could do for them, but what they could do for their country.

In the United States, at least, we citizens aren't government's customers. We're its owners. We seem to have collectively forgotten that fact.

It's a point the CEOs of cognitive enterprises should remember. To the extent members of the workforce think of themselves as owners, if not of the company itself then at least of the community that occupies the same space, the CEO will preside over a healthier community (next section), and therefore a healthier business.

They'll be bucking the trend. It's apparent that while people feel their community memberships in the social web keenly, even as they redefine what communities are (next section), as already pointed out their connection to their employers isn't as strong as it once was.

It's a trend worth bucking.

Communities

Wherever people congregate they form communities. This is no less true when the place they congregate is where they work for a living than when they go to a place of worship, a country club, or a local tavern.

Businesses are communities. Their executives have a lot of influence over the nature of the communities they lead, but no influence at all over the community's existence.

You might as well make the best of it.

In the 20th and earlier centuries, most communities were defined by proximity, stabilized by limited mobility, and buttressed by a shared culture and values that were enforced by peer pressure.

A community wasn't, of course, a single homogeneous entity. It was a hierarchy composed of households that aggregated into neighborhoods, neighborhoods that aggregated into regions, and regions that aggregated into towns and villages.

And they were not really a hierarchy either. Formally speaking, even then communities were networks. One's place of worship, for example, not one's religion, which was and is an entirely different matter, provided another community locus. It overlapped with the neighborhood or village but wasn't congruent with it.

Back in the 1980's, the bar or tavern you hung out at and your beverage of choice were important in this respect, too. The television show *Cheers* was something most viewers could relate to as just like their own experience only with snappier dialog.

20th century enterprises weren't all that different. They placed former strangers in proximity and the rest happened of its own accord. Businesses were and are communities as well.

A 20th century business was, for the most part, a hierarchy that at the smallest level started with workgroups, which aggregated into departments, which aggregated into divisions, which in turn aggregated into business units.

For departments and workgroups in particular, proximity was a convenience to make it easier to supervise, but from the perspective of social cohesion, proximity mattered more than departmental affinity.

Also like 20th century society, business communities were more networks than hierarchies. Those who practiced well-defined professions, for example, considered the local chapter of their professional societies to be communities they belonged to as well – communities that existed outside the business hierarchy.

That was the 20th century. In the 21st we've seen the rise of communities defined by affinities other than proximity – communities of interest, in particular, but also communities that are the result of social networks connected by means of social media.

In the 20th century, a family that didn't get along with its neighbors – often because they weren't like them – either moved or was intensely lonely.

In the 21st century if you don't get along with your neighbors you join one or more on-line communities of like-minded souls. In this day and age it isn't uncommon for people to have dozens of friends they've never met – friends just as close in their own way as their 20th-century in-person equivalents.

The roots of non-proximate communities go far back in time, of course. Probably starting with such communication technologies as drums and smoke signals, and later strengthened by postal services, other forms of community got started. Now, because of the Internet and its wide array of social sites as a driving force, communities are running rampant, bound by any of a variety of forms of shared interests and passions.

Green Bay Packer fans, for example, not only are a community, the team is owned by its community – a pre-Internet example, and if you don't like the Packers, try the Cubs and the team's Bleacher Bums, who throw any home run hit by the opposing team back onto the field.

Not a sports fan? Ravelry isn't just a website. It's a cohesive community of knitters and crotchetiers.

Those who post comments on *Keep the Joint Running*, the website run by one of this book's authors, are in many respects a community as well, as are those who post and tweet on countless other websites aimed at other topics of interest to other people.

The 21st century enterprise is entirely parallel. Members of its workforce take advantage of the multiple ways through which they form communities. Chapter 3 already explores one ramification of this radical change in how members of the workforce identify their affinities with each other: It' a driving force behind the increased permeability of business.

The trend: proximity-driven community is on the decline, while, driven by the increasing pervasiveness and embeddedness of technology, members of some communities have never met each other and in all likelihood never will. They belong to communities built around shared interests, and for all the ain't-it-awful-ism of Pleistocene commentators, it's hard to find a logical reason to fault people for preferring the company of those with whom they have a lot in common to those who happen to be physically nearby.

Before leaving this subject, a key point: The progression from family, to neighborhoods and places of worship, to communities, to the enterprise as a whole, results in a declining level of attachment … of we-ness, *we* being the source of all that's good and trustworthy in the world. That's as opposed to they-ness. You know, *them*. The ones who are stupid, evil, incompetent, have poor personal hygiene, and their mothers dress them funny.

We can be trusted. *They* can't. Communities represent the fuzzy psychological border that separates us from them.

The critical nature of *we*-ness is one reason large enterprises devolve into the dreaded organizational form known as *silos* instead of the more accurate term, "Success Prevention Units." We'll talk about SPUs and what to do about them in more depth in Chapter 9.

Meanwhile, consider this: Want a reason businesses should engage with their customers via social media? While it requires significant dexterity, done well it can at least put one or two of the organization's toes across that fuzzy border so the business becomes just a bit more "us" and a bit less "them," not to the extent the Packers, Cubs, and Apple have managed it, but to at least some extent.

Capabilities

Capabilities are what your business is good at. Not just what your executives, managers and workforce know how to do, but what the business as a whole is actually good at getting done.

In industrial enterprises, capabilities depend on infrastructure – such investments as buildings, assembly line equipment, supplier relationships, information technology, employee skills, process designs, and systems of management metrics.

Infrastructure is a critical competitive advantage for industrial enterprises. It's an investment that converts incremental and unpredictable transaction costs to predictable and invariant fixed costs.

But as Figure 6-1 illustrates, infrastructure investments have a downside. They create a huge level of inertia, because what infrastructure does is optimize a business for the business it's currently in, and freezes it there.

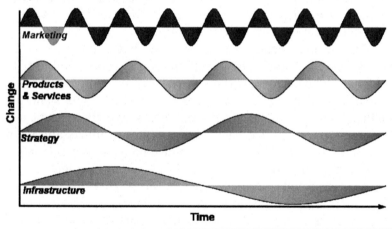

→ Marketing is about a company's products and services.
→ Companies base their decisions on what products and services to offer on strategy.
→ The business infrastructure enables and constrains strategy.

Figure 6-1. Infrastructure investments

This is just fine so long as the business your business is in today is similar to the business your business will be in tomorrow.

But as noted in Chapter 1, the stay-the-same/change ratio is shrinking, while adapt-infrastructure-to-business-change costs, cycle times and risks are not. So infrastructure outlasts, not just product lifetimes but whole business strategies, never mind the mayfly-short span of marketing campaigns.

Faced with the difficulty of infrastructure change, most businesses don't adopt the new strategy they'd most like to pursue, which means they don't offer the product lines they'd like to sell through the marketing channels they'd like to use to sell them.

Instead they choose their strategies based in large part on which ones the existing business infrastructure can adapt to.

This is, to say the least, a significant constraint.

Capabilities – the rise of craft

Industrial enterprises could invest in both physical and intellectual infrastructure. They could spend years building fixed factories, implementing large-scale software systems, and designing and perfecting operational business processes, confident the business strategies they supported would last long enough to profitably cover the cost of the investment.

Businesses executives could run the enterprise as a collection of processes staffed by a combination of robots and fungible employees who performed their work by rote.

But between the increased desire for unique goods and personalized service that's a consequence of wealth stratification (Chapter 1), and the decreasing longevity of products and whole strategies (the shrinking stay-the-same/change ratio), reliance on infrastructure-intensive, carefully designed and perfected business processes will be replaced by greater reliance on craft work.

"Craft" is an old-fashioned word. It describes a way of doing things that relies on individual skills, expertise, experience and judgment, along with relationships strong enough that no matter what the situation, everyone knows who to ask for help when their own skills, expertise and experience isn't up to the task.

Figure 6-2 shows the nature of this profound change. With traditional ways of organizing, craft work is just fine for small businesses, but traditional approaches to size bring with them the need to scale through infrastructure.

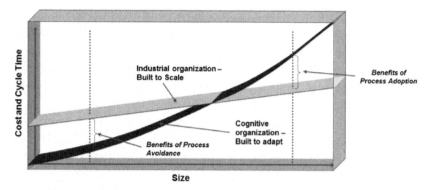

Figure 6.2 Scale through infrastructure

Cognitive enterprises will, in contrast, de-scale wherever possible, because the techniques needed for scaling always carry with them a need to dumb things down – a topic we'll take up in more depth in the next chapter. For now:

Infrastructure-supported industrial processes scale but are dumb – they're inflexible, built for repetition, reject customization and tailoring to different situations, and take great effort to adapt to changing circumstances.

Tools-supported crafts aren't optimized for scale. The reason is a matter of combinatorial math: The number of relationships between individuals in an organization is computed through the formula $n(n-1)/2$, which means the number of relationships to keep track of grows polynomially.

Craft-based processes rely on the intelligence, judgment, skills and experience of their practitioners. They rely on the relationships among practitioners as well.

That is, they rely on craft-based Communities.

Craft-based processing is highly adaptable and embraces customization and tailoring. Even better, because crafts require tools but not infrastructure, at low volumes of production they cost less in total than process-driven operations.

But craft, at least in its traditional forms, doesn't scale.

Is it possible to get the best of both worlds – adaptability at scale?

Without a doubt, the answer is a definite "sometimes."

One solution is to de-scale circumstances in a way that allows for craft-based processing. In the world of software development, for example, multi-year projects with large project teams has mostly given way to multi-year "programs," composed of multiple "initiatives," each of which has been broken down into a roadmap of small projects, typically no longer than six months each, with teams of no more than seven.

The other solution is to take advantage of the growing body of technologies designed to support communities. Taking a page from the social web, a growing number of businesses are experimenting with internal social media. If these attempts work, the result will be a two-fold advantage for craft-based processing: The internal social media will both turn individual knowledge into business knowledge – the essence of the cognitive enterprise – and they'll provide at least a measure of scale for the maintenance of communities of interest – another way of describing relationship-based crafts.

For now, let's leave it at this: For a growing number of businesses, leaders will have to find ways to either de-scale their circumstances or else make craft scale. Many of those ways will mostly start by thinking of the organization, not as a collection of processes, but as a collection of relationships.

They'll rely, that is, on communities and capabilities to take care of their customers far more than they'll rely on industrial-age processes, and expensive, infrastructure-oriented technologies. The people part of the old equation? Far from being an annoying impediment to change, it becomes the cognitive enterprise's greatest strength.

7. The end of the Industrial Process Panacea

"I don't have to practice. I'm good at it!"
— W. C. Fields, when asked if he practiced law

Canaries in the coal mine

Canary #1

Hard to believe but true: The Minneapolis/St. Paul metro area has more to offer tourists than just the Mall of America. One place to start (or at least it was way back in 1996) was a bus tour called the "RiverCity Trolley."

So here's your management challenge for the day: You have seven tour bus drivers hauling locals and tourists around the city's attractions. How do you design the drivers' spiel so as to delight your customers?

"Now let's see," you might be thinking. "To ensure quality we need to design a *process*. That's how you obtain repeatable, predictable results."

Or, you might be considering automation as a superior alternative. You could pre-record tour snippets with a professional announcer and link a digital player to a GPS so the system reads the right part of the script when the bus actually arrives at each point of interest.

Here's the solution David Wiggins, who ran the program for the Minnesota Historical Society, ended up creating. Quoting from the story in the *Star Tribune*, he gave the seven drivers, "... a stack of interesting materials about Minneapolis and let each one develop a personal tour. Some like the early history, some stress the contemporary. One knows architecture, another knows the music scene. Some try to be funny, some try to teach."

It's an industrial process consultant's nightmare: No well-defined series of steps; no process controls; not even a well-defined work product.

But that isn't the nightmare. The nightmare is that standardizing the process and supporting it with automation would have ruined the experience.

The Historical Society was able to offer a variety of customized experiences. For a business process consultant, that's the opportunity.

No, the sweet dream is that customers ... real paying customers ... gave the RiverCity Trolley high marks for fun, interest and value.

Canary #2

Not all that many years ago, one of us (RDL) was setting up a corporate apartment. My wife and I found an appropriate bed on the website of a retailer you'd recognize and placed the order.

A few minutes later we found a better bed for less from a different company. We placed that order and tried to cancel our first order on the retailer's website.

No luck.

So we called the customer service number. When we explained the situation and asked the nice woman who'd answered our call to cancel the order she explained that she couldn't. It had already been routed to the warehouse for fulfillment.

We suggested she call the warehouse to have them cancel the order. "I can't," she explained. "They don't have a telephone[12]."

Well, we explained, legally we had a three-day rescission period during which her company had to let us cancel the order without penalty. How, we asked, were we going to be able to do this?

Her answer: The warehouse would go ahead and ship the order. When it arrived at its destination, we were to reject the shipment. At this point UPS would ship it back to the warehouse at their expense.

Which is what happened. Except that by the time the bed arrived in New York its boxes were already battered, with a couple of holes deep enough to suggest it was damaged. By the time it ar-

---

[12] There's just no way anyone could make this stuff up.

rived back at the warehouse there's just no way it could have been anything other than a total loss.

Box score: Because the warehouse "had no telephone" the customer service agent couldn't improvise by calling; the warehouse staff couldn't improvise by rolling the bed from the shipping dock to the returns dock; and the company was out the cost of the bed plus the cost of shipping it, twice, from the warehouse to New York and back.

Efficiency can backfire.

Cognitive enterprises deal with Customers, Communities, and Capabilities. Customers come first because the first law of management is: *customers define value*. Real customers, that is – the ones who make buying decisions.

Quality, defined as the absence of defects, is certainly something customers value in a wide variety of circumstances, and to minimize defects there's nothing like a well-defined process supported by industrial-strength automation.

Customers don't, however, value quality equally in everything they buy. But unfortunately, like someone who only knows music in 3/4 time and so can only dance the waltz, many business pundits insist that designing and implementing well-defined processes is the solution no matter what tune the band is playing.

When you're manufacturing, which is to say when your goal is to create lots and lots of identical items, you do want repeatable, predictable results. By defining management goals for manufacturing in these terms the various process disciplines – Lean, Six Sigma, Theory of Constraints and even Business Process Reengineering (BPR) have led to dramatic improvements in mass-produced product quality worldwide.

But just like our 3/4 music lover and the waltz, many business thinkers believe all management problems can be reduced to building repeatable, predictable processes they can manage like a factory.

The problem isn't that this thinking is always wrong. The problem is that it isn't always right. As is so often the case when applying business theories, the challenge is to understand whether the theory fits the circumstances.

Take, for example, software development. The IT punditocracy has advocated creation of "software factories" for decades, on the grounds that the parallels between developing software modules and assembling automobiles are strong enough to carry the day.

When viewed from one angle, application development does look repetitive. How many times does IT have to design a database, program a bunch of data entry forms and reports, performance tune the whole schmear, and convert the old system's data before it's good at it?

But as *The Economist* once said, an analogy isn't the same thing as being the same thing.

When Ford manufactures Escapes, it wants every Escape in a particular batch to be absolutely identical to every other Escape made in the same batch. But when an IT software factory develops an information system, each software module is different, because what would be the point of developing multiple modules that do the same thing? Each software module IT creates is supposed to do something new and different or there would be no point to it.

The same may be said for any number of other business functions. Each advertising campaign ought to be different and unique. So should each new product design (hence "new and improved," even though nothing can actually be both new and improved).

Then there's project management – as explained in Chapter 1, the discipline businesses rely on to make change happen. As no two business changes are the same, project management can't be turned into a process in the industrial assembly line sense of the word either.

Industrial Processes vs. Practice

Compare bowling to hitting a pitched baseball.

It's easy to imagine a perfect bowling machine. Once you've figured out a speed, trajectory and spin that knocks down all the pins, all you have to do is calibrate the machine to release the ball with the right aim, velocity and rotation and you'll get a strike every time. The machine doesn't have to have any capabilities human bowlers don't have, other than consistency.

But hitting a pitched baseball? Calibrating a machine to swing the bat at exactly the same elevation, angle and speed will mostly result in building a machine that strikes out every time, because all the pitcher will have to do is throw the ball where the bat isn't. A perfect batting machine would have to determine a pitched ball's aim, velocity and spin, and in a fraction of a second use them to compute the ball's trajectory. With that information it could calculate the optimal timing, speed, elevation and direction with which to swing the bat.

In principle, at least, you can turn bowling into an industrial process. Repeatable, predictable results are the name of the game.

But you can't turn batting into a straightforward process, for the simple reason that the pitch you're trying to hit isn't predictable, and the reason it isn't predictable is that your opponents are doing everything possible to make it unpredictable.

Hitting a pitched baseball requires cognition or something very much like it.

That's how it is in every competitive sport – sports where you're playing against opponents, as opposed to sports like bowling and golf where you and your opponents are trying to do better when faced with identical situations.

The same is true in business situations where in order for you to win, a competitor has to lose.

Imagine, for example, an attorney whose courtroom tactics are 100% predictable. Is that who you'd want to represent you in a difficult case?

Of course not. 100% predictable means easy to anticipate, and easy to anticipate means easy to beat with the unexpected.

Which isn't to say lawyers just make everything up as they go along. Far from it. The law is a discipline with well-established ways of going about the work. The difference between what lawyers do and what assembly lines do is that for lawyers, following the defined series of steps isn't what wins the game. It's just the ante that lets you play.

Those who build assembly lines do everything possible to extract expertise from the minds of the experts who know how to accomplish what the assembly line is supposed to accomplish.

They build that knowledge into process steps, so that ideally, employees are fungible – cogs in the proverbial machine.

Lawyers don't follow a preset process. They engage in a *practice* – a craft – where the knowledge, expertise, skills and judgment of the practitioner are what make the difference between success and failure.

Industrial processes and practice are two ways to organize work. Each has its place. Nor are they alternatives. Think of them as the two poles of a continuum, for want of a better general term, call this the business function continuum, not as opposites.

Two points about business practices: (1) They've always been important; and (2) as the stay-the-same to change ratio shrinks, the practice to preset process ratio in business will increase.

Which brings up a nice irony: *Many business process consultants aren't aware that business process consulting is a practice, not a process.*

They won't even acknowledge the distinction.

Six dimensions of business function optimization

If you remember nothing else out of this entire book, remember this: When someone talks about optimizing an industrial business process, make sure they're specific about what they're optimizing it for. Turns out, you can optimize an industrial-age business process for at least one and not more than three of these six characteristics:

- *Fixed cost* – the cost of turning the lights on before any work gets done.
- *Incremental cost* – the cost of processing one more item.
- *Cycle time* – how much time elapses processing one item from start to finish.
- *Throughput* – how much work the function churns out in a unit of time; its capacity, in other words.
- *Quality* – the absence of defects.
- *Excellence* – flexibility, the ability to tailor to individual needs, and the presence of cool stuff.

There are those who will tell you they can improve all six. We've encountered these folks; some become quite vehement on the subject.

And they're right, in the sense that if the starting point is sufficiently dreadful, any schmuck can improve things across the board.

But most of the time, people just haven't been that stupid. And in any event, when designing how work should get done, there are intrinsic trade-offs among these dimensions.[13] For example:

- To reduce incremental costs, businesses generally have to invest in infrastructure, factories and information technology. These investments increase fixed costs.
- To improve quality, process designers almost always insist on standardizing work products. This is, by definition, a reduction in excellence.

A common way to improve throughput is to segment work into a larger number of shorter steps. This works, but at the expense of increased cycle time. In case this isn't clear, imagine a process with a single step that requires one hour of effort. Throughput is eight items per day, assuming an eight-hour workday.

1. Now, segment this step into a dozen steps. If for no other reason than that handoffs aren't instantaneous, each step will be longer than five minutes – make it six minutes per step with the newly organized process.
2. Throughput will be greatly improved. With each step handing off work in progress to the next step every six minutes, the final step will generate ten work products per hour – throughput is now 80 items per day compared to the original 8.
3. But cycle time has suffered – the original 60 minutes per item has been extended to 12 x 6 = 72 minutes per item.

---

[13] Chapter 3 of *Bare Bones Change Management* (Bob Lewis, 2010) contains an extensive exploration of these trade-offs.

When to uses industrial-age processes, when to use practices

Now that we have a vocabulary for talking about business function optimization, we can talk intelligently about when to organize work as an industrial-age process and when to organize it as a practice. As a general rule, **organize work as an industrial-age process to:** Reduce incremental cost; increase throughput, and improve quality. **Organize work as a practice to:** Reduce fixed costs; reduce cycle time; and increase the level of excellence.

The logic is straightforward so far as it goes. As already mentioned, processes require investments in infrastructure, and, to improve quality, they reduce complexity and customer choice with respect to work products. Also, by organizing work into some version of an assembly line, industrial-age processes achieve awesome throughput.

Practices rely more on the expertise, skills, knowledge and judgment of the practitioners (think adaptive case management and cognitive business process management). They require less infrastructure, meaning lower fixed costs. Cycle time is shorter because there are fewer steps and fewer handoffs, eliminating hand-off time and reducing the time work in process waits in an input queue.

And, they maximize flexibility, tailoring, and customization ... and therefore, customer choice ... because practitioners can apply their ingenuity to each situation as it comes up.

Here, then, is why practice, cognitive BPM, and adaptive case management will increase in importance relative to process:

Shorter stay-the-same to change ratios means that investing a lot of time and energy in the design, implementation and infrastructure required for implementing formal industrial-age business processes won't pay off. By the time the process is ready to rock and roll, the business will be too close to retiring it. You can implement business practices faster, because they rely on human beings figuring things out as the situation calls for it.

The rise of the luxury marketplace. Affluent customers who prize uniqueness while utterly rejecting the phrase "We can't do that for you" in conversations with sales or customer service –

customers like this mean excellence will be increasingly important as an optimization dimension throughout the enterprise's suite of business functions.

Project management is the discipline of making change happen in an organization, and project management is a practice, not a process.

Practice design

Even industrial-age businesses engage in a lot of work that is and should be organized as a practice. Examples include all forms of analysis, application development, insurance underwriting, loan processing, mortgage securitization, supply chain management, strategic planning, sales, copywriting, layout and design, recruiting, and, as mentioned several times already in this chapter, project management.

Perhaps someday you'll be able to draw on a body of knowledge for designing business practices that's parallel to what Lean, Six Sigma, and Theory of Constraints provide for business processes.

Until you can, here's a quick sketch of three basic ways to organize business practices – single-actor practices, hub-and-spoke practices, and team practices.

Single-actor practices

As the name implies, a single-actor practice is a way to organize work so that one person handles an assignment from start to finish. It includes such practices as financial analysis, copywriting, and project management.

Of these, project management has probably received the most attention, largely because managing large-scale projects has roughly the same success rate as the best baseball batters. If companies bat .333, they're matching the industry benchmark.

Strong project managers understand that their craft relies on a number of distinct activities. Some are more or less objective in nature, like project definition (defining the project objective, goals, and deliverables); planning (work breakdown structure, task estimates and interdependencies, resource planning); effort-tracking (time entry and tabulation; burn rate management); and progress tracking (task completions and critical-path management; preparing and distributing regular status reports).

Others require street smarts more than book smarts, like managing relationships with the business sponsor and key stakeholders; monitoring team dynamics and dealing with team dysfunction; and keeping an eye on team-member morale and taking steps to restore it when it starts to flag.

While there is a rough sequence to the activities project managers undertake – project definition generally precedes any need to monitor team morale, for example – project management isn't defined the way processes are defined, in terms of how to sequence activities and how to order the specific tasks that make up each activity.

Project management is defined by a large body of knowledge that provides guidance on how to handle the activities that make it up under a variety of real-world circumstances.

Hub-and-spoke practices

Imagine you're tasked with designing the claims-handling function for the life-insurance arm of a financial services company.

If you're belted in one of the standard process design disciplines you'll probably optimize it for low incremental cost, short cycle times, and high quality: Get it done, get it done cheaply, and don't make any mistakes in paying the claim.

Design claims processing this way and your client will unceremoniously throw you out on your ear, because for a financial services company, the demise of a life-insurance client is an opportunity to cultivate the investment and insurance business of the heirs. The more affluent the decedent, and the more complex their portfolio of insurance and investment products, the bigger the opportunity.

The flip side of this coin is a financial services imperative: Keep the money inside the company where it can continue to earn investment income – how life insurance companies make most of their profits.

For life insurance claims processing, the better optimization ranking is to put excellence first – the ability to tailor claims handling to the unique characteristics of each set of heirs. Quality probably follows closely on its heels, because when the decedent's heirs are ready to deal with financial matters they'll want accurate information about the decedent's estate.

Incremental cost probably comes in third.

A common way to organize claims processing is to assign a case manager to each claim. As with project management, claims management consists of a variety of activities (enumerating them is left as an exercise for the reader).

But where project managers handle management of each project as single actors, case managers are orchestrators – much of their job is to trigger various business processes and practices throughout the company, as needed based on the needs and dynamics of each individual claim.

It might involve opening a bank account, brokerage account or both to hold the proceeds of the decedent's portfolio until the heirs are ready to receive a distribution; it might involve assigning an investment advisor to work with one or more family members; it might even involve introducing the executor to a competent attorney to help with the details, if the executor is a family member who doesn't feel competent to personally handle the estate liquidation.

Not that the financial services company employs a stable of attorneys ready and waiting for these assignments. This is a simple referral from the case manager's network (if the financial services company doesn't provide the support it should) or from the financial services company's fully vetted network of approved estate management attorneys.

Much of the work triggered by case managers is work handled through industrial-strength business processes, for example, the liquidation of each item in the decedent's portfolio and the actual opening of various types of account.

But the orchestration of this work, and making sure everything gets done properly and on time, is a practice. Call it a "hub and spoke" practice, with the case manager acting as the hub, and each business function invoked by the case manager as a spoke.

Team practices

A team practice consists of, as the name implies, a team, composed of one or more individuals with the complementary skills needed to create the products the team is responsible for.

Software development is an obvious example of where team practices work very well – for specifics, look into the Scrum and Kanban software development methodologies. Software development teams typically will include a business analyst, developers, and software quality assurance specialists, with data designers, software architects and business subject matter experts on call when the team needs their expertise.

Many ad agencies also organize this way (if "organize" is ever an appropriate way to describe an ad agency), with teams composed of copywriters, layout and design artists (web and print), and an account manager, with specialists on call who can provide support for market research, media placement, search engine optimization, and so on.

The key to team practice design is that it assumes strong players in all roles, resulting in a very limited need for outside leadership. With a team practice, everyone knows what has to get done, and team members figure out who should do what so as to get it done.

Business Practices and the Cognitive Enterprise

Clearly, business practices are "smarter" than industrial-age business processes.

Industrial-age processes are black boxes. Other than their standard inputs they largely ignore changing conditions in the world outside the box because the whole point is to turn identical inputs into identical outputs, time after time after time.

That's in contrast to business practices, whose inputs aren't standardized (such as adaptive case management and cognitive Business Process Management (BPM)) and that are continually called on to adapt to changing circumstances. This is a big part of what cognition is for. As pointed out in the last chapter's discussion of OODA loops, it's about observing the situation, orienting to it, deciding what to do about it, and then carrying out the decision through disciplined, skilled action.

But if each practitioner does things completely differently from all other practitioners in the same role, the enterprise isn't cognitive at all. It's just a home for human beings who each practice their own, unique version of their craft.

Cognitive enterprises need ways to spread the knowledge, and even, at times, the good judgment of its best practitioners.

As mentioned in the previous chapter, part of the solution is to encourage the formation of communities of practice among the company's practitioners. It's an important beginning, but only the beginning.

A second part of the solution is to provide a standard set of tools to each practitioner. Not standard as in "this is all you can use," but standard as in a minimum collection each practitioner has at his or her disposal. And along with the tools comes training in how to use them.

Another piece of the puzzle is to develop easily navigated knowledge repositories. This is hard, because it asks practitioners to take time after doing their work to document what they did, how they did it, and why, and then to associate their documentation with suitable metadata so others can find it.

This is, by the way, one reason many business thinkers are pegging their hopes on internal social media: With Facebook, ETGers share far more of what they know, think, feel, and imagine than most of us want to have shared with us. That's in stark contrast to corporate knowledge management systems, most of which quickly develop the overall look and feel of a musty, disused library whose librarian is fighting a protracted case of the flu.

And, last of all, consider establishing apprenticeship programs. While the word has taken on Dickensian overtones, and in this day and age sounds utterly demeaning, it's actually an excellent, time-tested way for the inexperienced to learn a craft.

For the cognitive enterprise, apprenticeship programs just might be the perfect way to turn individual knowledge into enterprise knowledge.

Cognitive processes

The first iteration of General Motors OnStar had very little cognitive intelligence in its business processes. Service concierges wasted valuable time collecting information about the customer's current status that they often did not have in an emergency situation, and, for that matter, didn't need until after the emergency was resolved.

Rather than being satisfied with traditional call center scripting, the OnStar team designed the concept of "next best action" into its next-generation service offering. They designed its supporting information technology so that between the time the customer pressed the help button in the car and the service concierge answered the call, the concierge would receive every attribute about the driver's present status – attributes like the driver profile, location, local conditions, vehicle status and inferences regarding potential problems that might be the reason for the contact.

By having an accurate and complete analysis of the situation in near real time, OnStar's service concierges don't waste important seconds. They can begin solving the problem immediately. For example: "Hello Mr. Jones, it appears you are stopped on Interstate 95 in heavy traffic conditions. Your vehicle appears to be operating correctly, but you are towing a trailer. Does the trailer have a flat tire?"

The use of "next best action" recommendations demonstrates to customers that General Motors is there for them after the sale – the polar opposite of the traditional, simplification-driven, that-isn't-how-we-do-things-here approach that dominated industrial-age process design. Imagine if General Motors had adopted this sort of radical, mission-oriented, customer-value-driven thinking in the rest of its business.

Cognitive processes vs. traditional processes

Want to implement cognitive processes in your organization? Don't rely on industry experts. They've spent years developing mindless workflows, devoid of any intelligence.

This isn't a blamestorming session. It isn't their fault. It's just that they've been steeped in the techniques of industrial process design, which have an explicit goal of taking as much expertise as possible out of the heads of the employees who participate in it, embedding it in the process steps themselves.

That left them with two choices – make the processes so complicated you need genius employees to learn them, or enforce enough simplification that average schmoes can learn everything they need to know in no more than a couple of weeks.

Steeped in the practice of traditional business process modeling (BPM), designers were hamstrung with processes that provide only basic metrics such as: quantity purchased, orders processed or inventory remaining.

They call the result "industry best practice," embed their process designs in standardized software packages, and recommend that all corporations adapt to their process designs. They call it a "plain vanilla software implementation," and call it a day.

Actually, what they're calling a day is the minimum delay between process events and reporting on the metrics that are supposed to control them.

Imagine driving if the dashboard, rear-view mirror, and windshield of your car worked that way!

By the way, we are sympathetic. The bifurcated architecture used to generate business reports is difficult to escape from. When transactions are processed in one system and then asynchronously copied into a reporting system for measurement, the result is two repositories with built-in latency.

Without this architecture, though, resource-intensive reporting can drag the operational system's performance down to its knees.

And so, with only basic metrics available, traditional industry standard workflow processes such as order-to-cash, supply chain management or "human capital management" that are orchestrated in the transaction processing system were reduced to mechanized execution with little room for judgment, exception-handling, or improvisation.

Standardization requires less talent for execution, and so, as shown in the figure below, standard process design establishes a clear separation between processes, the people who work them and the technology used to automate many process steps.

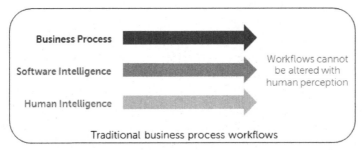

Figure 7-1 Traditional business process workflows

By contrast, cognitive business process design seeks to build adaptive, intelligent workflows through the integration of people, process and technology, not their separation.

Figure 7-2 Merging cognitive solutions

Think about flying a jetliner. Think about driving your car. Understanding a jetliner is much more complicated, if for no other reasons than that pilots have three dimensions, much higher speeds, and radar to contend with.

The process for flying a jetliner requires routine processes, with real-time instrumentation and skilled workers to accomplish its mission. It requires knowledge, perception, judgment and reasoning. The entire process is designed for "next best action" given the current circumstance.

Would you fly on a jetliner where the pilots had no knowledge of fuel consumption, air speed or altitude? Of course not. But workers in standardized business processes have only simple metrics, little room for taking the "next best action," and little or no "line of sight" to actual process goals. Their only option is to follow a predefined execution plan.

This is evident when you call a help desk, purchase a product or apply for job. They are all executed through mechanized business processes that have difficulty adapting to a changing environment, the changing environment in this case being you.

Cognitive business processes are designed to be adaptive. They require the ability to measure, decide and act independently to fulfill the desired outcome.

That's what OnStar did, by enabling the service concierge to solve customer issues without escalation.

Autonomous Solution Design

Whether you're designing a vehicle concierge service or the processes needed to fly a jetliner, the concepts required come from a field known as "autonomous solution design."

Most likely you aren't familiar with it. That's not surprising. It isn't well-known. But it should be, because unlike standard process design methodologies, autonomous solution design is intended for unpredictable scenarios.

We do, of course, use the term "autonomous" in business all the time, as in "they function as an autonomous business unit." We use it to describe entities that are self-managed.

Fundamental to business process modeling is defining the tasks each "resource"[14] is to perform. This is why, when you call a help desk, the automatic call distribution software prompts you to select billing, sales or support. It must route the call to the specific business unit or specialist responsible for handling the task in question.

The process has no intelligence to route the call without your input. It's not designed to be adaptive or autonomous. It's a workflow designed without information, which is why so many callers ask to speak to a "representative" – neither they nor the call routing software can figure out who they should be talking to.

Cognitive workflows would work differently. They have

---

[14] We use "resource" here in spite of its dehumanizing locution because the entity in question might be a human being but also might be a software module or robot.

"software agents" with the ability to observe, orient, decide, and act as autonomous "intelligent agents."

For a full account of agent-oriented BPM, read *Business Process Management: The Next Wave*.

www.mkpress.com/aoBPM

We'll use a call to a credit card help desk as an example.

When someone uses a credit card, a series of sensors and database look-ups assemble near-real-time data, such as the seller, transaction amount, date and time, location, and personal attributes. In modern companies, systems also monitor and incorporate relevant information from the social web (a non-trivial task but an increasingly important one).

A monitor gathers this "sensory data." When it detects an inbound help desk call it passes the information –transactional, database, and social-web-sourced – to an analytical engine, which looks for "tells." These are abnormalities from which inferences may be drawn, such as transactions taking place in a high crime area, coupled with the phone call originating from a mobile device located in an area distant from the cardholders' home zip code. The analytical engine reasons that this combination is likely to be a call for support because the credit card has been stolen while the cardholder is traveling.

Next, the analytical engine passes the analysis to the decision engine, which checks for the next best action from pre-built plans.

In the final step, the execution engine places the analysis, identity and recommendations on a dashboard and selects the next available service concierge with training in stolen-card handling. This specialist answers the call, greets the customer by name, confirms identity, confirms the problem really is a stolen credit card and that the card holder is traveling, and discusses what steps each party should take.

The cognitive process determined the cardholder is unlikely to be calling to get an automated read-out of their account status – most likely he/she has just been robbed.

If the call came from home and the transaction history was in the local postal code, the next best action would be different. The entire process unfolds in a split second from the time the monitor detect the help desk call to the time it answers it and dispatches it to an agent with execution instructions based on analysis of the current situation.

No prompts for process or language selection. No agents collecting information. No handoffs from one department to the next.

The cognitive process was designed to observe, orient, decide, and then act with intelligence.

And it's not just for customer service, but every part of your business.

Welcome to the cognitive enterprise!

The advances in process management
Source: www.mkpress.com/aoBPM

As written in the book, *Business Process Management: The*

Next Wave, "In a sense, the roots of modern management began with the arrival of scientific management in the 1920s and was dominated by Fredrick Taylor's, theory of management recorded in his 1911 monograph, The Principles of Scientific Management. Back then processes were implicit in work practices and not automated. In Peter Drucker's description, Frederick W. Taylor was the first man in recorded history who deemed work deserving of systematic observation and study. On Taylor's 'scientific management' rests, above all, the tremendous surge of affluence in the last seventy-five years which has lifted the working masses in the developed countries well above any level recorded before, even for the well-to-do. Taylor, though the Isaac Newton (or perhaps the Archimedes) of the science of work, laid only first foundations, however. Not much has been added to them since – even though he has been dead all of sixty years."

The First Wave. TQM. After WWII, applying science to process became front and center as W. Edwards Deming and Joseph Juran taught the Japanese about the power of quality management. Their work and the work of others triggered a wave of total quality management (TQM), spurred on by the publications of Deming and Juran in 1982 as shown below. The emphasis was not so much on the design of new processes, but on statistical measurements as a means of improving existing work practices and quality.

The Second Wave: BPR. Then a decade later, the 1992 blockbuster books, Process Innovation and Reengineering the Corporation, hit corporate board rooms, and reengineering work through information technology took off. In this second wave of business process management, processes were manually reengineered, and through a one-time, big-bang activity, cast in concrete in the bowels of today's automated Enterprise Resource Planning (ERP) and other packaged systems. Although "downsizing" is the moniker most remembered from Business Process Reengineering (BPR), it was technological enablement—including office automation—that allowed companies to tear down internal silos and reengineer end-to-end business processes that spanned individual functional departments (silos).

"Historically, ERP solutions had all the flexibility of wet concrete as they were configured and installed, then all the flexibility of dry concrete after installation. Even with document-centered workflow added to ERP, such systems only took up discrete roles as participants in processes; rarely did they provide management control over the processes. Those that did only did so for sub-processes and were generally limited in their capability.

The Third Wave: BPM. In the third wave of process management, the business process was freed from its concrete castings and made the central focus and basic building block of automation and business systems. Processes became first-class citizens in the world of automation. Change was the primary design goal because in the world of business process management: the ability to change is far more prized than the ability to create in the first place. It is through agile business process management that end-to-end processes can be monitored, continuously improved and optimized. Feedback of results, agility and adaptability are the bywords of the third wave.

The Next Wave: Agent-oriented Cognitive BPM. Both BPM technology and agent paradigms focus on addressing change and complexity. Intelligent agent technology is the next logical step in moving the BPM technology paradigm forward and overcoming some of its shortcomings. Both technologies have been around for quite a while but only now are they being repurposed for business in response to a rapidly changing world.

"The time has come where agents aren't just possible—they are needed to manage the growing chaos. In short, many companies will hit the wall if they stick to using conventional BPM Suites. Agents are necessary to scale—and 'manage chaos.' Agent technology provides support for BPM in a more flexible, distributed, scalable, timely, integrative, proactive, reactive, and intelligent manner—*intelligent processes*. The unfolding world of the Internet of Everything, is also a world of the 'Process of Everything,' and those processes will be built on *distributed intelligence*, distributed to each and every object with built-in cognitive capabilities to learn, think and act autonomously in a multi-agent environment of complex adaptive systems."

With the vocabulary introduced in this chapter it should be clear that cognitive processes have a lot in common with business *practices*, the primary difference being that cognitive processes rely on machine intelligence to replace or at least augment human judgment.

The dividing line isn't sharp and bright. A lot depends on how much time is available to set things up. The more time you have, the more machine intelligence you can devise.

A lot more depends on the stay-the-same/change ratio for the business function in question, because the way this will work in your business is that you'll set up all new business functions as practices first. As practitioners gain experience you'll add that experience to the constantly improving inference engine that supports next-best-action processing.

Exactly where the balance is struck between silicon and human information processing matters less than the ability to provide what customers increasingly demand. That's going beyond the absence of mistakes in their dealings with your company.

Customers will increasingly demand excellence. As the capabilities of information technology and the IT organizations that provide it increase, cognitive processes will likely prove to be your best way to deliver it at scale.

8. Industrial-Age IT vs. Cognitive-Age IT

"We'd all like to know how the information revolution eventually shakes out. I think we know. It ends in ordinariness, disappointment and advertising, as things always do." —T. Toles, *Washington Post*

Canary in the coal mine

Canary #1

Go to *Harvard Business Review's* website, www.hbr.org. Search for "HBR's 10 Must Reads: The Essentials." These contain, in the *HBR* editorial board's opinion, the ten most important ideas for business leaders it has ever published.

Interesting thing about these articles: The closest any of them come to even mentioning information technology is a piece on analytics.

The open question is this: Does the list fail to include anything about information technology because the *HBR* editorial board doesn't consider information technology important enough to include in its top 10 list. Or because its editorial board doesn't consider information technology to be important enough to have published anything about the subject that would warrant inclusion on its top 10 list?

Either way, it's clear *HBR* doesn't consider IT to be all that important to business.

One wonders if any member of its editorial board has tried running a business without it.

Canary #2

They just waved their wands and magical things happened.

My daughters ("me" being Bob Lewis) are allegedly adults now – allegedly because when we took a few days of vacation in Florida together, Harry Potter World at Universal Studios was at the top of their list.

In the Harry Potter books, and most books in which sorcery is an important part of the plot, magic doesn't involve millions of carefully designed and integrated bits and pieces. It's more a matter of opening your mind and exerting your will.

Which brings us to Harry Potter World. Give Universal credit. The attention it gave to detail is phenomenal, right down to selling butter beer (the preferred beverage among young witches and wizards at Hogwarts, I was informed). Which meant someone on the design team had to (1) recognize that selling butter beer would enrich the experience for Harry Potter fans; (2) persuade the budget-meister that formulating a recipe for butter beer and building places to buy it would be worth the investment; and (3) actually formulate a beverage that was palatable and had a flavor that tasted how something called butter beer ought to taste.

They also sold magic wands. Okay, they sold a lot of stuff – merchandising is part of the theme park equation – but at least they sold it in realistic Diagon Alley shops. In one, a master wand maker purveyed his wares.

Unlike in the books, exerting one's will and shouting something Latinish is optional. These wands have hidden circuitry and an infrared (I presume) tip. At various places in the park, if you stand in the right place and wave the tip at a discreetly positioned sensor in a shop window, something magical happens.

Nice touch. Huge crowds. The children (including my adult children, and, I confess, me too) got a kick out of it.

I'm willing to bet each and every visitor knew the effects were the result of technology, not magic, and could probably explain how they worked, at least in broad terms. Certainly, the park's designers would have known that once they described what they wanted, the engineers would have no trouble making it happen.

We aren't all members of the ETG (embedded technology generation if you haven't been paying attention) but we're all so accustomed to being enmeshed in technology that for the most part we only notice it when it isn't working right.

This is what's wrong with IT in a lot of companies – as a matter of fact, not blame or root causes. First, there's no butter-beer budget, to make sure users have a natural-seeming experience. And second, unlike Harry Potter World's designers, business managers in many companies are skeptical that if they describe what they're trying to accomplish, IT will deliver the technology needed to enable it without any trouble.

Welcome to the third age of information technology.

The first age was the age of the EDP high priesthood ("electronic data processing" is what we called it back then). The data center was its temple. Business supplicants came, hat in hand to ask the high priests for computer programs that could help them run their parts of the business. With the right burnt offerings the high priests might grant their requests, even as their acolytes, programmers (they hadn't graduated to being "developers" yet) and computer operators sneered at and complained about business users who were, they said, mere parasites on the system, much as greens keepers sneer and complain about the golfers who chop up their otherwise magnificent efforts.

The second age was the industrial age of computing. It was improvement of sorts, for everyone except the folks in MIS (management information systems) and then IS (the democratized version), stopped being arrogant high priests and started being shopkeepers – suppliers to their internal customers.

Then, to understand how to treat customers, they read Tom Peters and understood their mission wasn't merely to satisfy their customers but to delight them; a mission many IS professionals found irritating and some found downright worrisome.

Industrial-age computing pundits worked the internal-customer metaphor far past the point of utility, certain that because they could create correspondences between internal IT and a supplier, and between "the business" (as an internal supplier IT was not *part* of the business) and customers, that running IT *like* a business in every respect was the right answer no matter what the question.

Except that the folks who promoted this approach quite clearly understood nothing about business essentials. If IT really was supposed to be run like a business, its strategy would have been diversification and expansion of its customer base, and the prices for its products and services (billed and received through its chargeback system) would have been based on the law of supply and demand rather than on having to break even.

And it's even worse than that. In many companies that have chargeback systems so that IT's priorities really are whatever its customers are asking for, the CEO still insists on IT budget cuts. Not price cuts. Budget cuts. Which is somewhat less than entirely meaningful if IT is actually supposed to run itself like a business.

There is one more objection to the supplier/customer model of the relationship between IT and the rest of the business. Taken to its logical endpoint, it turns the entire enterprise into a marketplace of buyers and sellers.

Which might seem just fine, except for one minor detail. A marketplace has no purpose of its own. It's a space in which entities that do have purposes of their own try to achieve those purposes by trading and competing with each other.

Recall that successful businesses have both a mission and a business model, and try to reconcile that concept with business as marketplace. You might manage the mental contortions required to pull it off, but really, why would you want to?

And for the purposes of this book, business-as-marketplace is an anathema, because marketplaces, while they do have invisible hands, are not in any respect cognitive.

It's time to put these two extremes, IT as high priests and IT as lowly merchants, behind us. As business leaders recognize the value of making their organizations more cognitive, they'll increasingly insist on including IT as an essential and integral part of the organization.

Welcome to the third age of IT – the age in which IT is a peer and collaborator – an equal partner with the rest of business. It's IT as provider of technology leadership, and expert support for business executives and managers in their attempts to achieve intentional business change, thereby providing profitable value to the company's external, paying customers.

By the way, IT's third age isn't a consequence of the rise of the cognitive enterprise. Is it necessary for the rise of the cognitive enterprise? Probably. But dependent on it?

Not at all. It's been happening independently over the past

fifteen years or so, driven as much by the intrinsic limitations of the internal supplier/customer model of IT as anything else. It's still controversial in some circles, but that will pass.

This book isn't the place to talk about the third age of IT in detail.[15] Here we'll limit the discussion to the intersection of information technology, the IT organization, and the cognitive enterprise.

Information Technology and the Cognitive Enterprise

Ask your HR department for its standard performance appraisal form. If your company is like most companies, conspicuous by its absence will be mastery of the tools of the trade.

From the perspective of the cognitive enterprise this is only partially relevant. Because colleagues who are less than fully competent with a company's word processing, spreadsheet, presentation, and flowcharting tools, their decision to develop only rudimentary skills in such things affects only their performance, so long as their colleagues have mastered the art of responding to the request, "Hey, George, you're good with PowerPoint. Can you help me put some slides together?"

If George doesn't understand that, if he agrees, he's positioned himself as a technician and his colleague as a higher-level manager who knows how to delegate – shame on George.

But beyond mastery of personal productivity tools is mastery of tools that expand an individual employee's horizons – expand, the range of communities employees can be members of; expand their ability to discover the knowledge they need at the moment they need it; expand the range of colleagues with whom they can collaborate, and the effectiveness of their collaborations.

We now have tools that support collaboration among employees who are widely separated in space, time, and, as the chapter on enterprise permeability pointed out, the enterprise boundary as well – video calling, web conferencing, and support for co-authoring documents, including in real time.

---

[15] The right place to read about the third age of IT in detail is *Keep the Joint Running: A Manifesto for 21st Century Information Technology* (Bob Lewis, 2009).

Technologies exist that provide an inside-the-corporation equivalent of commercial social media, to support communities of common interests, and there are commercial websites that support inter-corporate communities of common interests as well.

Mastery of these tools – the ones supporting collaboration, community formation, and knowledge acquisition – is something few corporations appear to care about in the slightest.

And yet, having employees and partners collaborate no matter their longitudes and latitudes is increasingly essential to business success.

Meanwhile, it isn't only the ETG that's completely comfortable sharing knowledge and experience through the use of technology. Grandparents keep in touch with their families and friends on Facebook just as comfortably as teenagers share photos of the trips they've taken and parties they've attended.

Information Technology and the rise of business *practices*

In industrial-age companies, most of IT's efforts go into the support of operational business processes – they help make the steps repeatable and predictable through the automation of process steps and through the automation of their orchestration.

This doesn't come cheap, but then, it isn't supposed to. As pointed out in Chapter 7, it's in the nature of industrial-age processes that they have high fixed costs, much of which are the cost of the information technology needed to run them. In exchange, such processes get low incremental costs, which is to say they scale.

The systems that run industrial-age processes are coercive. In a very real sense, a company's employees report to them, as they tell employees what they should be working on and present the forms employees need to fill out to do their work.

Contrast that to the technology used to support business practices. Most of this technology comes in the form of general-purpose tools, like office suites, email systems, content management systems like SharePoint, web conferencing systems like WebEx, and innovative new process systems for Adaptive Case Management where the process is *emergent* vs. pre-defined.

Even specialized solutions such as project management systems are relatively inexpensive, and serve as flexible tools that support practitioners, not coercive workflow management systems that dictate the next step and how to perform it.

As pointed out in previous chapters, with the ever-shrinking stay-the-same to change ratio that is a primary driver of increased reliance on business practices rather than industrial-age processes, IT needs to develop an entirely new set of skills to properly provision and support the company's practitioners.

That's in contrast to the most common approach to such things, which, putting it kindly, might be described as the *Oliver Twist* approach, with practitioners of all stripes forced into the role of supplicant begging, "Please sir, might I have some more?"

Most IT shops, faced with budget pressures and security threats, have responded by keeping everything simple and then locking everything down so business users only have access to a minimalist set of tools that are carefully controlled by IT.

While understandable, these IT shops, along with the consultants and pundits who advise them, have all joined the Value Prevention Society (VPS). By focusing solely on cost and risk, they do everything they can to stifle initiative and creativity. The result? Those responsible for business practices end up doing just about everything on Excel. Excel is, in fact, a fine and versatile tool. But it isn't as versatile as specialized alternatives designed to support specific business practices, project management software being an excellent example.

Faced with the rise of business practices, industrial IT does the only thing it knows how to do. It says no. What should it be saying? Given how little practice-support systems cost when compared to traditional process management systems, IT should:

- Set up a curated software store containing applications that have been tested by IT or proven by other practitioners in the company, to save employees the trouble.
- Establish a standard, simple, secured, self-service platform for installing software that practitioners decide could help them and for reporting back their results so IT knows whether or not to add the software to the curated software store.
- Provide training and support for practitioners who want soft-

ware beyond the company standards so they know how to install what they think they need.

- Also provide a standard portal through which Software as a Service alternatives (SaaS, and if you aren't familiar with the term, this is the category Salesforce.com falls into) can function without compromising security, for practitioners who have selected a SaaS solution instead of installable software.

All things considered, the time and expense needed to support business practices is a small fraction of what's required to support traditional business processes, with low risk and high (although difficult to measure) returns.

And yet, most IT shops, trapped in their industrial-age perspective or forced there by industrial-age business executives, consider supporting mostly self-sufficient practitioners to be a low priority headache.

IT spending ratios and what to do about them

Take a look at Figure 8-1. It shows where IT spending goes. Most of it is "non-discretionary," which means that, in the short term at least, there isn't much to be done about it. It's money the business has to spend to turn the lights on and keep them on.

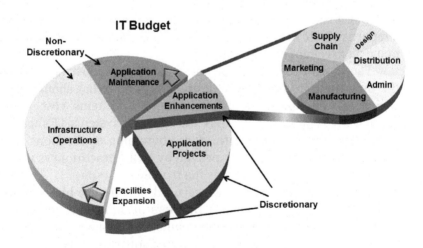

Figure 8-1. IT spending

True, some non-discretionary spending is akin to preventive maintenance. Strictly speaking, businesses can choose to not spend it, just as you can choose to not change the oil in your car.

But just as drivers who don't change the oil in their cars find out, there are really no savings to be had.

Pay it now or pay it later.

The rest of the IT spend goes to discretionary spending, which is to say, spending the company can choose to avoid or defer without doing itself any damage. Discretionary spending includes small software enhancements and growth-driven addition and expansion of facilities.

It also includes large so-called IT projects (really, the IT share of large business-change projects).

Large projects that include new information technology have an interesting characteristic. When they succeed, the software then has to be maintained, which requires additional staff, which further increases the non-discretionary share of the IT budget.

A rational response would be to recognize that IT is now delivering more value than it did before, which means it's logical to spend more to get that additional value.

The way most industrial-age businesses respond is to squeeze discretionary spending, on the theory that they're spending way too much on IT.

But trying to reduce overall spending by cutting the IT budget is like trying to cool a room by blowing cold air at the thermostat. The great thing about taking this approach is that the metrics will demonstrate success. The only thermometer in the room is, after all, built into the thermostat, so the metrics will "prove" the room is cooling down.

That the human beings in the room complain they're sweltering is irrelevant. They're just resistant to change; haven't they read *Who Moved My Cheese*?

Squint a bit at Figure 8-1 and you'll see something else in it. Non-discretionary spending is all connected to investments in the business as it is – investments in infrastructure. And as we saw in Chapter 6, business infrastructure doesn't change quickly. It outlasts business strategy, constraining choices. And, it eats into the budget and staff needed to support change and exploration.

And no, the cloud can't fix this. It can convert a company's capital investment in on-premise servers to operating costs in cloud computing licenses, but so what? What matters is that everyone in the company, inside and outside IT, has amassed considerable expertise in the company's information technology.

Which brings us to this. Shifting how work gets done from traditional business processes to business practices has the salutary effect of reducing the size of the infrastructure and the inertia it causes. It does so because of an interesting property of human beings. They're more adaptable than computers, and can be reconfigured to support other tasks more cheaply and easily.

The Pervasive Technology Era

Politicians tweet. Revolutionaries tweet. Even Tweety Bird tweets. Information technology did that.

Way back when, newspapers and television competed only indirectly, and not that much. Now, CNN.com and Washington Post.com compete for the exact same advertising dollars and news consumers. Information technology did that, too.

The Arab spring has turned, sadly, into a chaos of constantly aligning and re-aligning factions. But it started with courageous people, linked through the use of cell phones and social media. Technology might not be what made the Arab spring happen, but the Arab spring probably couldn't have happened without it.

In the world, information technology has become embedded. It's integrated – Facebook, Twitter, Spotify, YouTube, Pinterest, World of Warcraft, Flickr, Skype, not to mention Word, Excel, PowerPoint, and of course Google. These aren't Things People Learn. They're part of the landscape.

This wasn't the case twenty years ago, but it is the case now.

In much of the business world, information technology is a separate category of spending.

How did the world get so far ahead of the business world? How is it that in the world, information technology is embedded and integrated, while most business executives continue to think there's such a thing as an "IT project?"

If you work for one of them, or if you work for a CIO who works for one of them, give it the old college try one more time, by explaining the point about IT as value enabler.

Right now, the trend-spotting community is hot on the trail of something variously called "the digital transformation," the "third platform" and, among the cynical, "everything that's trendy blended into a casserole." It's the combination of (in no particular order) social media, cloud computing, big data, the next-generation workforce, smart products, the "internet of things," and mobile computing.

But most of those writing about the subject are still trapped in the old there-is-such-a-thing-as-an-IT-project perspective of things.

The transformation is more fundamental than that. It's all of the above, viewed from a 90-degree angle. It's the world of business when IT isn't a case-by-case decision anymore – information technology is, and is expected to be, pervasive.

Understand, this transformation, no matter what name you give it, is an aspirational vision, not a practical reality. Right now, implementing each component in a way that's integrated into the business requires a lot of heavy lifting – in digital transformation land there's no equivalent to buying an ERP system that delivers it all in a coherent, integrated package. And if there was, we'd probably revisit the tired old plain-vanilla vs. customization arguments that tie so many ERP implementations in knots.

We're not advocating a full-steam-ahead approach, if-there's-a-computer-involved-somewhere-approve-the-project approach to business investment governance. That would be both unaffordable and stupid.

The situation is both simpler and more complicated than that. It starts by changing the hidden assumptions of the business.

Hidden assumptions have power – more power than evidence, than logic, than the formal axioms and postulates required for mathematical and geometric proofs.

We use them to reach conclusions just as surely as Pythagoras relied on the parallel postulate, and because they're unconscious we don't know we've based our decisions on them.

Take the ETG, the embedded technology generation. As pointed out in the Prolog, the ETG stands one of IT's cherished hidden assumptions on its head, namely that your average employees paint Wite-Out® on their computer monitors to correct word processing mistakes.

So listen up. The ETG has never heard of Wite-Out®. And while very few generational generalizations hold up to even the shallowest scrutiny, this one does. Your average member of the ETG doesn't think twice about learning new technology or new user interfaces. That's assumed, and often fun.

There's a reason the iPad never came with an instruction manual, and it isn't that the iPad's user interface is so intuitively obvious that anyone who picks one up automatically knows what to do with it.

Nope. It's that the iPad's early adopters figured they could figure it out by just poking around, and anything they couldn't figure out that way they could Google, just as they can Google cheat codes for a game if they get stuck.

Apple understood this mentality and took advantage of it. That's Apple's hidden assumption.

Your average IT shop, on the other hand, is built on the assumption, the hidden assumption, of widespread employee technophobia.

Where this assumption does partially stand up is in many companies' executive suites.

Understand, this isn't because the executives in question are stupid or ignorant. It's because they only understand social media, big data analytics, mobile, and all the rest in their heads. That is, they can and often do understand the evidence and logic supporting their importance.

But they don't get it in their gut.

Here's what we mean: In his groundbreaking *Thinking, Fast and Slow,* Daniel Kanneman explained where non-linear-logic-based thinking is entirely reliable, and even preferred. The perfect example: recognizing people you know. You don't need to create a logical narrative to prove the person you're looking at is your old friend Frank. You recognize Frank's face and that's that.

For you, that is. If you want to prove it's Frank to someone else, that's when you need to produce his driver's license.

Few corporate executives are members of the ETG, and as a result they need the driver's license. They don't have an internal picture of how it all hangs together and makes easy sense. No matter how receptive they might be to the idea that, for example, an internal social media site will do more for knowledge sharing than a Knowledge Management System, they can't live the reality the same way they recognize a face.

Shadow IT and the Integration Partner Organization

In the era of pervasive technology, information technology is the default assumption. And yet, even two pundits who don't have to deal with the day-to-day budget constraints you live with all the time have to acknowledge that your IT organization will never have enough bandwidth to make technology as pervasive as it needs to be.

Enter so-called "shadow IT," information technology that's implemented without the involvement of an Information Technology organization.

The whole notion of shadow IT horrifies IT traditionalists, who, in spite of considering the rest of the business to be their customers, think more like dieticians than restaurateurs. In case the point isn't clear, if IT was serving food instead of managing servers, it would suggest, pointedly, "Aren't you a bit chubby to be ordering the porterhouse? I think you'd be much better off with the Cobb salad," instead of asking, "Would you like the baked potato, smashed potatoes, or French fries?"

Or, changing metaphors, imagine going into Home Depot to buy some drywall, only to have one of the sales associates explain, "Oh, we won't sell you that. You aren't qualified. We only provide this to our installation teams. Want to talk to them?"

Fortunately, in the third age of information technology there are no internal customers. IT is a peer and collaborator in designing, planning and implementing intentional business change.

But still, IT's attempts to stop shadow IT are like squeezing a closed tube of toothpaste. The toothpaste just moves around inside the tube, just as shadow IT is moving from the PC's hard drive to the cloud.

IT used to be able to pretend. It would lock down the desktops, hoist up the landlubbers, and everyone would congratulate each other over having followed security best practices.

It's time to stop pretending. Once upon a time, IT could prevent the sales force from installing Act! on their laptops, thereby reducing an already-minor security risk while helping make sure the company's revenues were smaller than they could have been.

That was then. This is now. IT can still lock down their laptops, but it can't lock down the cloud, which means that while IT can stop the sales force from buying Act! licenses ($550 each one-time). The only way to stop them from "installing" Salesforce.com licenses ($780/year ongoing) is to use a website blocker, which means the cost of blocking Salesforce.com (blockers aren't free, and someone needs to administer them too) probably exceeds the cost of buying Act! licenses.

The killer? The usual cant about Software as a Service is how much more economical it is than the usual IT-installed solutions.

But never mind the cost. Mind instead this uncomfortable fact. If the sales manager wants sales force automation (now incorrectly called "CRM"), he or she can contract directly with Salesforce and have CRM through everyone's browser, no IT involved.

Entirely equivalent statements may be made about every other manager in the company, either by licensing a SaaS solution or by contracting with one to develop a custom solution that's hosted in the cloud, but also accessed via a standard Internet browser.

Imagine that instead of trying to stamp out shadow IT, IT embraced it. The sales director would have explained that many of the sales reps wanted to install Act! Is there any problem with this?

No. No problemo, so long as they're willing to be self-supporting (just as they are with Salesforce.com) and aren't looking to integrate Act! into any of the company's other systems.

And if Sales wants IT to provide integration and support? That also isn't a problem, and costs the same whether IT is integrating and supporting Act! or Salesforce.com.

There are three bottom-line "goods" in any business: Revenue, cost, and risk. Stamp out shadow IT and you'll reduce risk a bit. Embrace it and you help improve revenue and cost.

Tough choice.

Which gets us to the true nature of 3rd-era IT: The meaning of the "I" has changed. "Information" Technology was always something of a strange name. Where it came from was the high price of database management systems, back when the CIO (the head of electronic data processing back then) was trying to justify buying one of the early ones. About the only internal sales pitch that convinced the company's top executives was that the information these things managed was so insanely valuable that the seemingly insane high price of the technology needed to manage it made actual sense.

That was then and this is now. Acquiring and installing systems that support actual work is becoming easy enough that business managers don't need IT to help them with it. Configuring them to support work the way the business manager would like it to be done? Still far from easy, but an outside vendor can provide the same sort of help IT can provide, and the outside vendor has already specialized in whatever package it is the business manager has selected.

Welcome back to the islands of automation IT has been wrestling to the ground for the past two decades, because when a business manager selects and implements a software package without benefit of IT, that's just what's been created: an island of automation.

The CEO is trying to make the enterprise cognitive, which requires that knowledge be sharable everywhere, and in the meantime, through the magic of shadow IT and the cloud, the information required to develop that knowledge is increasingly fragmented.

But wait! There's more!

Integrating the un-integratable

Once upon a time, a period of time lasting from the dawn of computers to, more or less, last week, when IT had to integrate the information from two systems it matched unique or nearly unique information in equivalent records from the two systems.[16]

---

[16] This is, as it happens, a hideous oversimplification, but for our purposes

A customer's social security number used to be a popular choice for all the obvious reasons, although the rise of identity theft has reduced its appeal.

Now, whether the knowledge a company's decision makers needs is about its customers, its products, or its employees, a good bit of it resides outside the company's walls, in various forms of social media.

Knowing a previously good customer is likely to defect is handy information for companies smart enough to take advantage of it. So is knowing that a good customer is about to add to the family, to buy a car, or to otherwise experience a "life event."

Knowing your new product stinks in the eyes of your customers is also handy knowledge to have, especially if their complaints are specific and in rough consensus.

Knowing your employees and contractors all hate you, the company you lead, and the horses you and your fellow executives rode in on might not be the most comfortable bit of knowledge you've ever had to deal with, but it's handy knowledge nonetheless. And because its source is their online conversations with their friends and family it's a lot more reliable than what you get from your annual employee satisfaction survey.

It's handy knowledge in the aggregate. It's even handier when correlated with the quality of the employees making the complaints. That chronic underperformers complain isn't particularly disturbing, or interesting. But if the company's star performers are saying this, it isn't just more interesting. It also helps the CEO spot bad managers who are poisoning the community well, and to find ways to reach out to the star performers to try to persuade them to stick around for a while.

Integrating information from social media with information from your internal systems is, to say the least, not a solved problem. Moreover, it isn't a problem an individual manager, contracting with a SaaS vendor or custom developer can solve, because individual managers can't and shouldn't be able to expose the company's internal databases to outsiders.

---

here it will do.

Over the years, large numbers of business pundits have predicted the end of IT because of how one panacea after another was going to make it all as easy as Tinker Toys®. The need for IT is, because of these wondrous tools, supposed to go away.

The cloud is just the latest of these panaceas.

The Big Finish

Welcome to the future of IT. It's a future in which the "I" no longer stands for "information." It now stands for "integration" and the department's name will be "Integration Partner" or something that says as much. IP's most important job will be integrating disparate systems, some of which it implements itself, some of which happens though shadow IT projects (which, it should go without saying by now, are really business change projects that have no shadows in sight), and some of which are the ever-evolving swarm of social media.

The evolution of Information Technology to Integration Partner won't be smooth and simple, in particular because not all of the critical skills needed to make this happen have been codified yet.

On the other hand, for CIOs (that's right: Chief Integration Officers) whose heads are screwed on straight, that's what will make it fun.

9. Leading a Cognitive Enterprise

"A good leader inspires other men and women with confidence. A great leader inspires them with confidence in themselves."
—Eleanor Roosevelt

Canary #1

Then came the blizzard.

It happened like this. One of us ("I" for the rest of this tale of woe) bought round trip tickets to New York City. A week after that trip I'd booked a long weekend in Florida with my parents.

Then plans changed and I had to stay in New York an extra week, which meant I'd fly to Minnesota Thursday evening to get on a flight to Florida the next morning. The fare rules, you see, didn't allow converting two round-trip tickets into one triangle fare.

Then, the day before I was to return to Minnesota, the weather service forecast snow there, and lots of it. The airline cancelled my flight in anticipation and rebooked me for the following morning, to arrive a half-hour after my flight to Florida was scheduled to depart.

I called customer service, explained the situation, and suggested that under the circumstances, routing me directly to Florida clearly made more sense for both of us.

But the fare rules still wouldn't allow it. The best the airline's customer service representative could do was to rebook my Florida flight to later in the day. I asked him to check with his supervisor, which he did. No go. She wouldn't or couldn't override the system. "I guess I'd better speak to your supervisor, then," I suggested. He connected me.

"I know you have complex fare rules that mere mortals like me can't fully comprehend." I began. Those were the last words I would successfully utter for at least five minutes.

The customer service supervisor scolded me, that's a mild

164

description, for (1) being disrespectful to the airline; (2) trying to game their fares to get a cheaper flight to Florida; and (3) now trying to cheat to get the best of both worlds.

I confess that by the end of the call I became somewhat testy. Anyway, the next morning I spoke to a different supervisor, described my previous attempt at resolution, and asked if the airline really wanted to fly me in and out of a blizzard zone when a simple and easy alternative was staring both of us in the face.

She told me the first supervisor had placed a red flag in my records. It said that under no circumstances should anyone help me out. When I asked who I should write to file a complaint about the first supervisor she suggested a *quid pro quo*. The first supervisor, she explained, was really a very nice person but had clearly been under a lot of stress. If I'd agree not to write a complaint, she would take care of me.

So I didn't and she did.

Canary #2

Once upon a time, one of us had a manufacturing client.

The CEO, wanting a well-run company with clear lines of accountability, divided the business into functional responsibilities: Sales and Marketing, Supply Chain, Manufacturing, Distribution, and Administration – support functions like accounting, HR and IT.

He appointed an executive to run each area. He established financial incentives for each, based on clearly defined metrics, which he had read were Best Practices.

Each month, he reviewed the company's financial reports, expecting to see dramatic improvements.

Here's what happened instead:

Sales and Marketing did well, delivering profitable contracts. The Senior Vice President, Sales and Marketing, was content.

Supply Chain did a phenomenal job of procuring raw materials. Unit costs were significantly lower than they had been, and the Senior Vice President, Supply Chain was justifiably proud of her department's performance.

Manufacturing's performance was phenomenal, too. The factory's utilization ratio was well over 95% and unit costs for finished goods were even lower, compared to previous years, than those of raw materials. The Senior Vice President, Manufacturing complimented his team and waited for his bonus check.

Distribution's performance was also very good. It was a model of efficiency – delivery costs were lower than the previous year in spite of increases in the cost of fuel and labor. This made the Senior Vice President, Distribution smile.

Then, Sales and Marketing began receiving complaints from customers. Depending on the customer, and the month, they sometimes ran out of inventory and sometimes received such large shipments that they couldn't fit everything into their warehouses. If Sales and Marketing couldn't fix the situation, they threatened to take their business elsewhere.

The Senior Vice President, Sales and Marketing complained to the Senior Vice President, Distribution, who responded like this: "Let me get this straight – you're asking me to sacrifice my bonus check to help you solve a problem? Why would I want to do that? And even if I could, I couldn't anyway. Manufacturing gives me product according to its production schedule. I can't ship what I don't have, and I have to ship what I do have so it doesn't clog our warehouse."

So Sales and Marketing complained to the CEO, who tried to fix the problem by realigning responsibilities. He placed responsibility for the production schedule in the hands of Sales and Marketing. That, thought the CEO, should fix that.

What happened instead was that the factory's utilization ratio plummeted. It sat idle for significant periods of time, and failed to deliver on the production schedule created by Sales and Marketing. The reason? Frequently, the factory didn't have the raw materials needed for what the production schedule called for. Supply Chain wasn't providing them. It shopped for price.

That led the Senior Vice President, Manufacturing to complain to the Senior Vice President, Supply Chain, who explained that in order to receive raw materials based on the manufacturing schedule, the company would have to pay more. Many small batches are more expensive than a few big ones. With her bonus at stake, the Senior Vice President, Supply Chain wasn't willing to do this. Why would she?

> That's when the CEO really did fix the problem – not by another realignment, reorganization, or yelling, but by changing what he paid bonuses for.

"We have too many managers and not enough ... LEADERS!"

It's a common, if misguided complaint. Only James Earl Jones can say it right, "Shorn of the mystic aura and suggestions of genetic innateness that so often envelop discussions of this subject, leadership in business is a tool of management far more than the reverse."

Disagree? How about this? Management is the art of getting work out the door. It's about results.

Leadership is the art of getting people to go where you want them to go, of getting them to follow, willingly and even enthusiastically, under their own steam and providing their own motivation.

In business, what matters is getting work out the door.

Which isn't to minimize the critical role leadership plays. It's a vital skill for managers because of the old, old joke about the guy who owned a dog with no legs. Every morning he had to take it out for a drag.

Management in the absence of leadership is a drag for everyone involved. It's a drag for managers because they have to provide all the energy. It's a drag for employees because it makes going to work a lot like being just one of the dogs pulling a sled, with no say in the destination or route, and with all the usual comments about what the view is like when you aren't the lead dog.

In an earlier book,[17] one of your authors broke leadership down into eight tasks: Setting direction, delegation, staffing, making decisions, motivating employees, building teams, defining culture, and communication. All eight are learnable skills, which means that while not everyone can become a great leader, any manager can become a better leader.

Surrounding all of these tasks and giving them context is a core principle. While managers get the work out the door, leaders

---

[17] *Leading IT: <Still> the Toughest Job in the World*, Bob Lewis, 2011

build organizations that can get the work out the door by the usual and standard means when they fit the situation, and by improvising and figuring things out when they don't. That is to say, leaders build organizations designed to succeed.

This has always mattered. If you want to lead a cognitive enterprise it matters a whole lot more.

This chapter will focus on four aspects of the cognitive transformation that aren't covered elsewhere: the difference between accountability and responsibility; a behavioral trait called "followership;" the increasing impact of organizational silos and what to do about them; and the pre-eminent importance of the business culture.

Accountability vs. Responsibility

Holding employees accountable has always been a terrible idea, but it used to be one business leaders could get away with. Given the forces buffeting companies right now, the ones described in the early chapters of this book, it's a concept that's simply too flawed to be allowed to continue. Executives who want to run a cognitive enterprise have to let it go.

But hey, wait a minute. Isn't holding employees accountable a good thing? You probably read something to that effect in the *Harvard Business Review* at one time or another and it sounded pleasing. Muscular. Authoritative.

And yes, it does sound that way. But inevitably, it turns out to be a game of Whack-A-Mole.® It's only outcomes are to:

- *Create a blame-oriented business culture*, because when something goes wrong and you hold someone accountable, you're deciding whose fault the problem is.
- *Make sure the root cause never gets fixed* because when you hold people accountable you've already decided what the root cause is – someone didn't do what they were supposed to do. This means the root cause was not a problem with systems, processes, or a decision you yourself made upstream.
- *Prevent initiative*, because if, when something fails to go right, your response is to assign blame, who in their right mind would voluntarily try to deal with a situation instead of keeping his or her head down?

168

- *Make employees stupid,* because that's one of the predictable consequences of fear – it gives people energy, but blocks their cognitive processes.
- *Keep you ignorant* of everything you most need to know about, because if you're going to hold someone accountable for a problem, they'll do their best to make sure you don't find out about it.
- *Keep the whole organization ignorant* for much the same reason: Who's going to share their knowledge and collaborate in conditions like this?

Encouraging the habit of taking responsibility

You want employees to take responsibility. No matter how carefully you hire, some employees who don't have this habit will slip through. Or you might inherit some.

What do you do about it?

Give them a chance to fail.

That is: Delegate assignments for which success is possible but not easy.

Delegate well, which means you don't just toss the assignment on their desk and then walk away – you provide regular coaching and support.

But you don't un-delegate and you don't specify how to do things.

The employee has to be able to fail. Because for an employee who doesn't have the habit of success, the experience of success is intoxicating. It feels amazing.

It's a feeling that employee is going to want to experience again.

And the only way to get to success when you're in a position where you might fail is to take personal responsibility for the assignment.

It's a great feeling.

Isn't it?

Oh, and one more thing: When your approach to managing employees is to hold them accountable it reduces your obligation to attract, recruit, retain, and promote the best talent you can find. After all, by holding them accountable you're taking more responsibility for their performance, meaning they're less responsi-

169

ble for it, or at least, they'll deserve less credit for it.

If you still aren't convinced, there's a good chance you're confusing holding people accountable with insisting employees take responsibility. The two are frequently conflated, but they're polar opposites.

When someone holds an employee accountable the employee's motivation comes from the outside – a fear of unpleasant consequences.

Taking responsibility, in contrast, is internal – something the best employees do because that's how they're wired. Only that isn't an entirely fair statement, because taking responsibility isn't innate. It's a virtue that can be taught, encouraged, and learned.

Employees who take responsibility operate on their own steam. It's the ones you have to hold accountable you have to take out for a drag.

One more thing. If you have employees you have to hold accountable it means you hired the wrong employees, or failed to address bad hires made by your predecessor. Do you want to be held accountable for that, or would you prefer to take responsibility?

In industrial-age business theory it was okay to hire employees who were merely adequate and hold them accountable, because old-school businesses relied on processes, procedures and policies to make sure everyone knew what they were supposed to do, and what they weren't permitted to do.

And that was okay, because industrial-age businesses had plenty of time to deploy processes that were just good enough, and learn their way into them.

Now? With the shrinking stay-the-same/change ratio, by the time many companies have learned their way into their current situation, they're busy moving on to what's next. There just isn't time to perfect processes anymore, because they don't last long enough.

The balance has shifted, from needing good-enough employees working inside great processes to great employees who consider current processes and practices to be just part of their working toolkit.

Who you employ has always been more important than how

you organize your processes. The proof: No matter how bad your processes, great employees will find a way to get the job done, but no matter how great your processes are, bad employees will always find a way to cause them to fail.

Q.E.D.

All that changes when you want to lead a cognitive enterprise is that your situation is more like it was than it ever has been.

If you need any more convincing, how about the financial payoff? If you have to hold employees accountable you'll need enough managers to know enough about what they've been doing to hold them accountable. But if you hire employees who take responsibility, you need only enough managers to make sure everyone knows what's expected of them.

That's less expensive, which everyone running a business knows is a Good Thing.

What does this have to do with running a cognitive enterprise? Everything. Because an organization built on the concept of holding people accountable is one in which everyone keeps their heads down, which means nobody is sharing what they know. It's too dangerous. It's also the opposite of a cognitive enterprise where, you'll recall, the organization "knows" what its workforce knows; that is, knowledge is shared widely.

People who take responsibility will ask each other for help, and they'll give their help when asked.

They'll find the knowledge they need to succeed because that's one of the ways successful people succeed.

Followership

You lead. Others follow. It's a parade. Parades are good.

Even better: You find a parade and run to get in front of it. You call it leading the parade; everyone in the parade is too busy doing their part to argue. It's even better because once you get in front, the only energy you have to expend is staying in front.

No dragging. No amputee dogs.

You're a business leader. Compare two situations. In the first, everything flows through you. You have the most complete knowledge, the all-encompassing perspective, and the best judgment. Not that you disrespect everyone else's expertise. It's just

171

that they have their jobs to do; your job is to make the key decisions and direct traffic.

The second situation: You have an empowered workforce, with decisions "pushed down" as far as possible. No waiting in line for your attention. Decisions at the speed of thought. Pick your glorious metaphor and apply it here.

What you want is for everyone in the enterprise to think of themselves as leaders within the enterprise, "leader" defined as we're defining it here – as anyone good at getting others to follow their lead. Except for Figure 9-1.

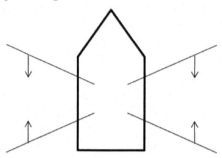

Figure 9-2. Trireme (simplified) where rowers in front and back disagree about the direction.

It's vector algebra at its simplest. Imagine you're captain of an ancient Greek trireme. You encourage leadership wherever you can find it. And so, you end up, quite by random accident, with two strong natural leaders. One sits toward the front of the boat, the other toward the back. The one who sits forward believes passionately that Forward Ho! is the right way to go. The one toward the rear is just as forcefully convinced that Go Back! Is the right answer.

And so, the oarsmen in front pull their oars as hard as possible to move your boat forward. The ones toward the read push theirs just as hard to move your boat backward.

The result is a lot of energy expended while your trireme floats in one place, immobilized by the intense effort.

There's only one solution: Reorganize! So you move your two strong leaders so that one sits on the left side of the trireme, the other on the right. Their opinions, though, haven't changed. It's just that now it's the oarsmen on the left who try to move the boat forward while those on the right try to move it in the other direction (Figure 9-2).

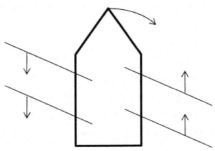

Figure 9-3. Reorganized trireme (simplified) - rowers on right and left-hand sides of the boat disagree.

New result, though. Instead of sitting motionless, you spin in a circle. You still aren't going anywhere, but now your head spins, right along with the boat.

Not a blinding insight, but still a critical one: If you want to run a healthy enterprise, its strongest leaders need to have a shared sense of direction. Their agreement doesn't have to be slavish and precise. Just close enough to keep the boat that is your enterprise from churning in one place or spinning in circles.

With a shared sense of direction, every leader in the enterprise adds more impact. The word for this form of leadership is "followership" – following the leader's direction without needing much in the way of guidance.

Why is an enterprise with more followership more cognitive? Same answer as before: For followership to happen, knowledge has to be widely shared so that everyone in a leadership role understands not just where the business is going, but why that's where it's going and how the different parts of the business will need to collaborate to get it there.

The cognitive enterprise vs. the siloed enterprise

Figure 9-3 shows the usual view of a company's organizational chart.

173

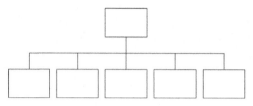

Figure 9-4. Org chart, standard view

What it shows is who reports to whom. When employees look at it, though, they often translate it to what it really shows (Figure 9-4) – boxes within boxes within boxes.

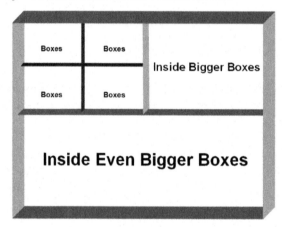

Figure 9-5. Org chart - employee view

It's a perfect picture of what my job isn't. It's also a fine representation of the extent to where another group in the company falls in the continuum that has one pole labeled "us" and the other pole labeled "them."

Few business executives say they want their organization to devolve into silos. Strange thing though: Based on our experience as management consultants, silo-ism is the rule rather than the exception in most businesses today, and the best response many executives can muster is to scold everyone for turning the company into a bunch of walled off rival fiefdoms.

Which says they either don't know the root causes of silo-ism or consider the cure to be worse than the disease.

One root cause: Workforce members at all levels, from individual contributors through top executives, have no reason to care about the success of the company as a whole, and plenty of reason to care about the success of their little corner of the world.

Another source of silo-ism comes from people losing track of what they have in common, paying more attention on their differences instead. Often this comes from the alignment of professional communities with the org chart: Accountants who work in Accounting have a reinforced sense of who else belongs to the trusted group known as "us," which easily turns into a reinforced sense of who isn't a member of the group. The rest of the company becomes "them," whether *they* are the bureaucrats in HR, the propeller-heads in IT, or the crazies in Marketing. And the feeling toward the bean-counters in Accounting is mutual.

The perfectly natural tendency people have to divide the world into *us* and *them* causes everyone to lose their ability to solve shared problems – the reason an earlier chapter called them Success Prevention Units.

It's a paradox: In a business ecosystem in which organizations are increasingly permeable, the silos inside the organization become impermeable.

As the hallmark of the cognitive enterprise is widely shared knowledge, silos have to go, or at least receive a lot less emphasis. Even more important, employees' sense of competition has to stop being directed at the department down the hall instead of at their counterparts in your fiercest rival in the marketplace.

At the risk of pushing a metaphor too hard, this is akin to advising that the Great State of Texas should focus its job-growth efforts on taking business, and jobs, away from China and Germany rather than outcompeting Wisconsin and Nebraska.

Where might an executive start the process of de-siloing the enterprise? Start with a different image than boxes within boxes – an image like Figure 9-5.

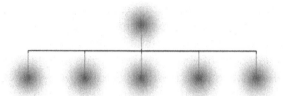

Figure 9-6. Org Chart, cognitive view

The difference between a traditional org chart and the attitude fostered by the image in Figure 9-5 is that Figure 9-5 represents the org chart as areas of focus, not limits of responsibility. The heart of each organizational unit is clear, but there are no hard boundaries.

The whole theory of traditional organizational design is that business management is supposed to define the boundaries of each organizational unit, along with clear interfaces and such. It's as if the enterprise is a computer program with each organizational unit serving the role of a subroutine[18] – closed and encapsulated, exposing only its inputs and outputs.

That's how everyone knows what they're accountable for.

The flaw is obvious to anyone who's ever tried to design the perfect organizational chart, namely, there is no such thing. No matter how you design an organization, there's always going to be a lot of important effort that doesn't fit within a department's boundaries. Honest charts cannot be drawn without dotted lines, and lots of them.

As a general rule, operational responsibilities fit inside a traditional org chart. But just about every important decision does not. Important decisions almost always require collaboration.

Go back to the second canary that opened this chapter and ask yourself, which organizational unit should have authority over the manufacturing schedule? Sales, which is in the best position to balance the needs of different customers? Or manufacturing, which is in the best position to maximize capital utilization? Or Supply Chain, which is in the best position to minimize the cost of raw materials?

---

[18] Or if you're a more modern programmer, objects and services.

Or take a responsibility as fundamental to the business as product development. No one department can own it. Successful product development requires collaboration among design, engineering, supply chain, marketing, manufacturing, sales,[19] even IT. All have important contributions to make, and they're best made as peers and collaborators, "cross-functional" teams, aligned to a shared purpose and whose members trust each other.

More or less the opposite of how traditional org charts tell people to behave.

The question is how leaders can combat the natural tendency people have to coalesce into distrustful tribes. The answer is, first unwind everything the company does to encourage the coalescence. Second, do everything possible to prevent their recurrence.

What encourages silo formation: A short list

- *Communication must flow through the chain of command:* If Jill in Marketing isn't allowed to talk with Greg in Engineering until the path has first been cleared through communications up the chain, this is simply ridiculous. It doesn't happen as much as it used to happen. But it still does happen, and except for high-security need-to-know situations, it's ludicrous.
- *Calling it the "chain of command":* What a horrible name. It says the entire management structure exists to take a high-level edict (command) and flow it down through the organization so everyone knows about it and is properly obedient. Need a different name for it? It's your company's management structure.
- *The compensation system:* More often than not the compensation system is designed as the penultimate enforcement mechanism for holding people accountable. If they don't get the job done they don't get a raise or annual bonus; if they do, they do.
  Which would be fine if "getting the job done" was assessed in terms of collaborative get-the-job-done-doing. But usually, it's assessed solely within the boundaries of everyone's assigned

---

[19] How many companies engage the sales force when designing the products they'll have to sell? Answer: Too few.

organizational unit.

Companies pay people to form silos and stay within them.

- **Excessive reliance on specialists:** Almost by definition, specialists live within silos because you hired them for their in-silo expertise. Add to that the natural sense of kinship specialists have with others who share their specialty, and voila! A silo is born.

  Take a look at your recruiting practices. In contrast to entrepreneurships, which rely on creative generalists to figure things out, most large organizations segment responsibilities narrowly in order to field deep expertise.

  Which is just fine, right up until the point that it isn't fine anymore because nobody is left who can assemble the specialists' pointillist views of the enterprise into a complete picture.

  When everyone's view is narrow, all you can have organizationally is silos, and the best you can achieve when it comes to designs and decisions is one incoherent compromise after another.

- **Managerial reliance on exclusivity as a motivator:** Exclusivity is one of the five great motivators – marketing motivators that is, the others being fear, greed, guilt, and the need for approval.

  Some of these can be effective motivators for business leaders as well, especially the need (or at least desire for) approval. So, for that matter, can exclusivity when used properly.

  Exclusivity is taking pride in being part of an elite team. It's probably derived from the insecurity of being just one out of roughly 3.5 billion adult human beings, which does make one feel less than irreplaceable.

  Used properly, exclusivity means comparing your team's performance to parallel teams in competing companies. As too-often used, it means ridiculing a rival department down the hall. Either form of exclusivity has the salutary effect of motivating better within-silo trust, coherence, and as a result, performance. But this raises the silo walls even higher, preventing collaboration wherever it's used.

- **Ignoring outside competitors:** Speaking of interdepartmental rivalry, when we talk with clients about business strategy, we're constantly astonished at how little attention most pay to competitors.

Oh, there's lip service in the generic "grow marketshare" sense, but where is the sense to say "here are our top three competitors, here's our plan to take business away from them," and "here's our plan to keep them from taking business away from us." Not so much.

At least in U.S. culture, competition comes naturally. Fail to establish a competition *ethos* and your employees will find convenient targets for competition inside the halls of your business.

- **Ignoring independent staff:** This, you'll recall, is one of the trends explored in the first chapter. Businesses prefer contract staff to employees because they require less paperwork and are easier to shed when times get tough or needs shift to different skills, experience and expertise. Nor is this unilateral. Increasingly, members of the workforce prefer the flexibility and meritocracy that independence brings.

  Along with all of this comes a complete lack of loyalty to anything beyond the project independent staff are assigned to. Because what other loyalty could they possibly have? They're being paid to help bring *this one project* in on time, within budget, and with all of the planned deliverables intact.

  Want them to broaden their horizons, to keep a broader context in mind? To do what's best for the enterprise as a whole, even if it means de-emphasizing their project?

  You can. But that takes leadership too. Just because a member of your workforce is independent, that doesn't mean they're independent of the need for leadership.

Breaking down silos and keeping them broken down

Business leaders can't eliminate silos by eliminating all of the factors that lead to their formation. Getting rid of the organizational chart, for example, is a non-starter: No matter how much is changing in the business ecosystem, every business needs to organize so everyone knows who is supposed to do what, when, and in which order.

Here are the ones you can do something about:

Followership: Start with Figure 9-5. Start with everyone in your company who has a leadership role. Now mix in a sense of followership, where everyone in the company is a leader of the company, with a shared sense of direction and purpose.

Just a different area of current focus.

Compensation: There's a mistaken idea that the compensation system is a system of financial incentives. It's a dreadful idea. We aren't the first to point out that this amounts to thinking you have to bribe your employees to put in their best efforts and to do what's best for the company[20].

Thinking of the compensation system as a collection of financial incentives is dangerous, but thinking of it as the company's loudest voice for communicating what it values is right on, you'll pardon the expression, the money.

And so many compensation systems shout "FORM SILOS!" at the top of the company's lungs that no amount of counterargument in other channels is likely to have much of an impact. Which leads to this simple formulation: Create opportunities for employees, and especially for managers to collaborate. More than opportunities; situations where the only path to success is collaboration.

Then compensate for those results.

Take advantage of the competition: It's a rare company that exists without competitors. These unlucky few are called monopolies, and they have a difficult time of it, because with competitors there's always another hill to climb. Without them all the company has to do is satisfy the regulators.

With competitors, organizations have to constantly stretch. Without them, all the organization has to do is to continue to be just barely good enough.

Recognize your competitors. Celebrate them. Let everyone in the company know, you expect them to beat the competition, no matter which part of the company they work in.

If everyone is trying to beat the competition they'll be far less likely to try to beat each other up.

---

[20] Original source: *Punished by Rewards,* Alfie Kohn. Full discussion in *Leading IT: <Still>The Toughest Job in the World*, Bob Lewis.

This isn't a book about business strategy per se. It's a book about how businesses can succeed at whatever their strategy is. Here, one suggestion: ***Make your strategy be about beating other companies.***

This is actually quite radical – most tracts on business strategy have, for decades, emphasized the desirability of avoiding competition through unique positioning.

But trying to avoid competition through unique positioning invites more aggressive companies to eat you alive, while it invites members of your own workforce to compete with each other.

Which might explain why so many once-successful corporate giants are felled by audacious start-ups that strategize to win instead of strategizing to avoid playing the game. Three recent examples illustrate the point: Barnes and Noble, demolished by Amazon; Blackberry, destroyed by Apple; the Yellow Pages, wiped out by Google (you didn't realize Google Maps is the new Yellow Pages?).

From the perspective of organizational silos and what to do about them, what matters is this: In most enterprises, most employees, most of the time, direct most of their competitive energies to beating the department down the hall, not their counterparts in outside competitors.

From the perspective of making your enterprise more cognitive, the strategies and tactics a company pursues to beat a competitor call for smart, coordinated action – the essence of the cognitive enterprise.

Required collaboration: Back in the industrial era, Management By Objectives (MBO) was popular. It has fallen out of fashion for the most part, at least as a name and formal theory, but the basic notion: Assign goals to each manager and hold them accountable for achieving them, usually by making their bonuses dependent on achieving their goals. The result: Instant Silo, because *my* job is to achieve *my* goals. If a laser beam focus on this isn't going to make the whole company better, that's Someone Else's Problem.

But what happens if you assign each goal to two managers instead? If each manager has three goals each year, each manager has three separate collaborations to make happen. Silos are less likely to drive decision-making under these circumstances, and that's without taking into account how much each manager will learn about the three other areas led by the managers they're now required to collaborate with.

Cross-functional teams: Just as requiring managers to collaborate removes the incentive to create silos, so placing staff-level employees in situations that require them to collaborate eliminates a lot of the social forces that drive silo formation, namely, the easy tendency to divide the world into "us" and "them."

A cross-functional team turns a lot of people who used to be "them" to each other and creates a new "we" they all belong to.

Distrust has a hard time surviving in situations where people have to depend on each other to get the job done.

Culture

Now for a too-short discussion of an enormous subject: the business culture.

The standard model of how business works is PROCESS/technology/*people*, which are placeholders for how work gets done (process), the tools required to execute process steps (technology) and the skills, knowledge and experience needed to fulfill process roles (people).

There's broad acknowledgement that cultural change is often a critical dimension of organizational change management, but it's a supporting role, not the lead story – part of how to minimize resistance to a given change.

Even with old-school business change, this was probably inside out, because it was never a good idea to tailor culture on a process by process basis – add it to the list of how to raise silo walls even higher.

For leaders who envision the shared knowledge and unified goal-adoption of a cognitive enterprise, on the other hand, culture is the core consistency – the unifying force that pulls everything else into line.

Culture as infrastructure

Culture is rooted in shared assumptions. These assumptions can come from anywhere, but they're best if they're based on actual knowledge.

Which brings us to a profound understanding of just how important this all is. To the cognitive enterprise, **culture and the shared knowledge it depends on is part of the business infrastructure.**

In the cognitive enterprise it's the heart of the business infrastructure. Infrastructure is what changes the most slowly in any business. It supports some potential strategies and places severe constraints on others. Businesses rightly invest significantly into their infrastructure because of its impact on how well they're able to execute their business model, and when culture turns out to be an impediment to a desirable future strategy, effective business leaders recognize the need to invest in a change-out of its constraining elements.

As a leader of a cognitive enterprise, think of the business culture and the shared knowledge on which it's built as infrastructure investments.

It's a perspective that will serve you well.

The nature of culture

But we're getting ahead of ourselves, because *culture* is one of those words that's easy to slip into a conversation but hard to pin down to a specific meaning.

For our purposes, we'll use three definitions, each useful in different contexts.

The first comes from the branch of anthropology where it was defined as *the learned behavior people exhibit in response to their environment.*

Not, by the way, behavior in the procedural sense. "When someone calls the help desk with a problem, we first open a ticket," is not an account of culture.

"When a crisis arises we don't worry about the org chart. We all pitch in, figure out what needs to be done, and fix the problem," that's a description of a cultural trait.

This anthropological definition is operationally useful, because you can use it to engineer the culture. More on that in a moment. But before that, the second definition, which is useful because it's simple.

Culture is how we do things around here.

George Burns, asked about sex at age 100, described it as like trying to play pool with a rope. Trying to make change happen, any change, in an organization with the wrong culture is like that too. With a culture that's compatible with what you want the organization to do, making the change happen is like pulling the rope instead of pushing it. You might have to pull harder some times than others, but that's just work.

It isn't all that difficult anymore, because – well, because that's how we do things around here.

The third definition of culture is in many ways the most important. It's how people throughout the company define *us* and *them*.

Engineering culture

By our operational definition, culture is the learned behavior people exhibit in response to their environment.

To change the culture you have two alternatives – either change the environment people have to respond to, or change how they respond.

We trust you won't need a lot of convincing to accept that, human beings being the pesky critters that they are, changing the environment is easier.

Except for this. In an organization, most of the environment people experience is the behavior of the people around them, more so in a traditional office environment, less so with remote employees, but even remote employees don't exist in a pure task-assignment/fulfillment situation, and the better they're managed the less isolated they feel.

So to change the culture you have to change the behavior people exhibit in response to the behavior people exhibit in response to the behavior people exhibit.

This is one reason cultures tend to stabilize – they're the result of reinforcing feedback loops.

But it isn't hopeless, because not all of the behaviors people respond to with their own behavior are created equal. Leader behavior has an outsize impact on culture. Want to change the culture? Change leader behavior. Starting with your own. If there's something about the culture you don't like, it's a good bet leader behavior is the root cause.

To engineer the business culture, think about broad situations that matter. Decide how you want employees to behave in them. That's the easy part.

Here's the hard part: Figuring out what you and your fellow business leaders are doing that discourages the behavior you want and encourages some other behavior you don't like half as much. And, next, figuring out what, as leaders, you need to do instead.

There's a lot more to cultural engineering than this scratch-the-surface account. This book isn't the place for the deep dive, though the aforementioned *Leading IT* is. [21]

And in conclusion ...

Once you start thinking of your job as a business executive in terms of encouraging and fostering a cognitive enterprise it redirects your attention in dozens of ways. It broadens how you think of goals, purpose and strategy. It changes how you spend your time and energy. It redefines what you consider success to be.

The phrase "engaged workforce" is rapidly becoming a cliché, and it's too bad, because highly engaged workforces really do outcompete apathetic ones – the ones who are only there for the paycheck, trading an honest day's work for it.

The cognitive enterprise is, in some respects, a way of looking at the engaged workforce through the right side of the telescope.

The notion of an engaged workforce is that employees are committed to the organization's goals and work tirelessly to help you accomplish them.

A cognitive enterprise acts like an entity that has purpose,

---

[21] Don't worry about the title. Most of the book is about leadership no matter what sort of organization you're leading.

and uses its fund of knowledge and awareness of its environment to make intelligent decisions. Without employees, and not only employees, but independent staff too, who are committed to the organization itself there's no way the business will ever behave like that.

It's an old-fashioned notion. Quaint, perhaps. Leaders of cognitive enterprises will have to give up a lot of recent intellectual baggage because when you want your workforce to be committed to the enterprise's mission and purpose. You really can't at the same time operate from an attitude of employee fungibility and disposability.

It's okay. It's time. And why would you want to hire fungible and disposable people anyway?

10: The Way Forward is a Slippery Slope

Canaries

In 2011, IBM's artificial intelligence (AI) system Watson beat the best of Jeopardy's previous winners. And in fact, it didn't just beat them. It beat the metaphorical pants off them.

In 2014, Google bought a company called DeepMind. Deep-Mind had invented a new game-playing AI system. The way it worked was that it connected its AI up to 49 different old Atari video games. It wired it up to the game controllers and gave it a view of the screen with no instructions on how to interpret the pixels, other than teaching it where on the screen it could find the score.

With nothing but this information, and the instruction "max-imize the score," the AI taught *itself* to beat every one of the games, playing far beyond the level of their best human players.

Also in 2014, a Japanese venture capital firm named Deep Knowledge put an artificial intelligence system on its board of di-rectors. It made the decision because Vital (the name given the AI system) supposedly picks up on market trends "not immediately obvious to humans."

"Nobody owns the customer, but someone can always own the moment."—Scott Hudgins, VP, Walt Disney Company

The cognitive enterprise is more human than its industrial predecessor – more human because it's based on knowledge, judgment and values shared by the human beings who comprise the enterprise.

That's in contrast to the current situation, in which humans act as the corporation's agents. The current situation is dehuman-izing because, as pointed out in the first chapter, the corporation is an entirely different species from us and an amoral one at that.

Acting as an agent for an inhuman, amoral entity might be

profitable, but it's hardly the stuff on which enthusiasm is built.

But even assuming that participating in a cognitive enterprise will be more humanizing (or at least, less dehumanizing) than in an industrial one, that doesn't make the benefit intrinsic. It's more a happy accident, and there's no guarantee that in the future, cognitive enterprises might become just as dehumanizing in their own way as the industrial enterprise is right now.

How it turns out won't be a matter of undirected evolution. It will be the result of some conscious choices we need to start making right now. And in fact the business community has been making them; probably not as wisely as it might.

The big issue is how information technology, and the business use of information technology, will evolve.

Enterprise Architecture

The golden rule of design is *form follows function*. It's one of those rules that is obvious once stated. You can't successfully design solutions until you fully understand the problem you're trying to solve.

In this case, the question is how to design a cognitive (or any other) enterprise.

What follows on one of the most commonly used frameworks for designing, building and implementing businesses and the processes, practices, and information technology solutions they rely on. It's known as TOGAF (The Open Group Architecture Framework), and while it's neither better nor worse than any other such framework, it has the benefit of being familiar and well-tested.

In case you aren't familiar with it, TOGAF uses a modular four-level approach to design (Figure 10-1) that starts with business processes (layer #1, but in this book modified to distinguish between traditional processes, practices, and cognitive processes).

Business processes are underpinned by applications, data, and platforms (also known as technical infrastructure).

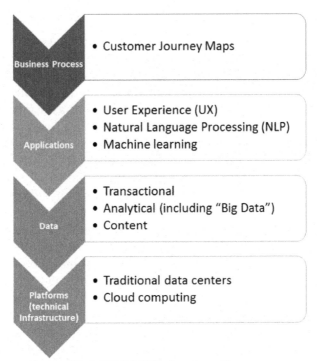

Figure10-1. TOGAF Technology Taxonomy

The formula for the cognitive enterprise is Customers/ Communities/ Capabilities. So it makes sense to start with customers, and in particular with a concept called "journey mapping," a method for designing how you want customers to experience your company.

Journey mapping defines how you manage the relationship between your customers and your organization as they move through various stages of the engagement lifecycle.

What's most significant about journey mapping is its emphasis on "touch points" – that is, each interaction a customer has with your organization, its intent and purpose from your customers' perspective, the opportunity it provides to cement your relationship, and the risk it imposes for damaging it.

Each touch point also provides an opportunity to gather more data about a customer, adding to the organization's knowledge, thereby allowing it to provide more value and serve that customer better.[22]

The next stage in the TOGAF progression is user experience design (UXD). UXD analyzes user interfaces at every touchpoint for maximum customer enjoyment, efficiency, and effectiveness.

While UXD has been part of the IT landscape since punch cards gave way to interactive terminals, UXD as a formal discipline (and acronym) first gelled in the world of mobile applications. For our purposes this is vastly insufficient. Cognitive enterprises orchestrate user experiences within and across all customer touch points. They also pay attention to the variety of devices through which customers interact with them, including not only mobile devices and personal computers, but also something as prosaic as the telephone and the interactive voice response systems that might or might not be used to answer customer calls.

One more bit of complexity: UXD isn't limited to technology. Many of the most important touch points in a journey map are with the men and women who work in and for your business, not directly with information technology. This human UXD may involve formal scripting, but also might provide for less-structured conversations. Behind it is usually an application UXD optimized to support these human beings as they provide the touchpoint described in the journey map.

Whatever the touch point and channel, an important aspect of UXD is the information architecture that underpins it. It must both provide the data, scratch that, it must provide the *knowledge* required to provide the desired customer experience, while collecting additional data for use in later touch points.

User experience design focuses on a personal engagement philosophy, which means the practices and cognitive processes it creates will depend on extensive knowledge about the customer, and must be able to adapt on the fly to changes in the relationship.

To support a more cognitive user experience, the application architecture makes use of two more technologies. From a purist's perspective they are *platforms,* used in building applications. To-

---

22 Translation: Sell that customer goods and services he/she is more likely to want.

gether they transform IT from a warehouse of data to a purveyor of knowledge in the data/ information/ knowledge/ judgment/ wisdom sense of the term – the DIKJW pyramid explored earlier.

The first of the technologies is the ability to communicate in ordinary spoken language (the buzz phrase is "natural language processing," NLP for short). If you own an Apple iPhone you experience NLP firsthand with its "Siri" concierge agent.

Siri is the kid sister of IBM's Watson – the system that beat all human comers on Jeopardy. "She" can't actually hear your voice, of course. Siri encodes your speech and transmits it to servers in the cloud (that's the second technology) for analysis with tools that perform natural language processing. Once the request is parsed and evaluated, the tools formulate a suitable response – perhaps by searching and evaluating information on likely websites, or by using a mapping engine to calculate a driving route, or by summarizing user reviews of nearby restaurants on the social web. This backend system then encodes the response, packages it, and sends it back to Siri, which speaks it to you.

The Siri system has one more capability – it learns, and so improves over time. Along with Watson, Siri's learning algorithms let it move beyond providing data and information. In an admittedly primitive way, Siri delivers knowledge in the DIKJW pyramid sense.

The final technology in the modern information landscape is the ubiquitous compute layer called cloud computing. Ignore most of what you've read about it. Its value is badly misunderstood.

The usual story is that cloud computing costs less than what companies install in their data centers. It doesn't, and even if it did, cost is less important than capability and construction when IT assembles the platform layer of the techniques architecture.

The complete explanation of what the cloud is and isn't suitable for is complex, and not particularly relevant to creating a cognitive enterprise.

What matters here is that Siri operates on a sophisticated computing platform, the iPhone, which has limited resources. If the original Siri had to rely only on the phone's processor, memory and network, it would have taken hours just to parse the language.

Processing power has increased since then, to the point that Android's speech recognition engine now runs in the phone. But there's a lot more processing needed to understand and answer a question than is needed to recognize its words. It's through the cloud that enough of the right kind of processing can be brought to bear to provide answers, from wherever the questioner asks a question.

Progressive: Using technology to make the business smarter

Add another pair of technologies to the NLP and cloud computing mix: smart products, which, when coupled with the Internet of Things (IoT), make companies smarter, which is to say, more cognitive.

First and foremost, smart products are cooler products. Adding processing power to things makes them more interesting things.

Add to that the ability for products to send information back to the mother ship (the IoT) and you get something roughly akin to how your five senses send important information back to your brain. Smart products and the IoT can provide cognitive enterprises with contextual awareness. Contextual awareness is essential for any entity to exhibit judgment, whether we're talking about a wolf, a human being, or a cognitive enterprise.

Example: For years, car insurers have known that it's the driving habits of the individual that establish actual driving risk. It didn't matter – all that the insurers could actually feed into their actuarial tables were traffic tickets, recent accidents, and a few demographic characteristics that correlated with higher accident rates.

The fact about driving risk is that bad things happen to good drivers through no fault of their own. But on average, worse things happen to the reckless.

The challenge: Insurers had no reliable way to recognize actual reckless driving, as opposed to drivers who, statistically, are more likely to be reckless.

In 2011, Progressive Insurance closed that gap by designing

a device that plugs into a vehicle's diagnostic port. It transmits a continuous stream of data describing actual driving behavior in real time: acceleration, braking, and lateral cornering. It's real time telemetry transmitted from the snapshot device in the diagnostic port to an application on the driver's mobile phone that shares the data with Progressive. The result: Actual safe driving results in a discount.

It's technology that makes Progressive more knowledgeable about its customers. Not just some of its employees. Progressive the business is smarter. Which is to say, more cognitive than it was before.

If this was limited to Progressive it would be nothing more than an illustrative anecdote.

But of course, imitation being the sincerest form of flattery, insurers in all lines around the world are applying this model to such risk areas as plumbing – to prevent losses from burst pipes – and wearable devices that track kinetic movement to assess life insurance risk.

And the fun is just beginning. The potential for cheap processing and communication (smart devices) connected to back-end analytics processing (that's using the IoT to connect to a cloud-based analytics environment) gives businesses enormous potential to understand each individual customer in ways that create both enormous potential value, and a vastly improved ability to explain that value in terms that make the most sense to each message recipient.

It's a blueprint for *cognitive* solution design.

But just because something is profitable, that doesn't mean it's always a good idea.

For an excellent account of where cognitive computing is headed, read *Cognitive Computing: A Brief Guide for Game Changers* (Peter Fingar and Vint Cerf) and visit the associated Web site, Cognitive Trends. The book is a briefing of just 78 information packed pages, but contains QR codes and links for readers who want to drill down on various topics. The Web site contains news, articles, books and videos.

Who ... or what ... will be in charge?

Canary #1 was Watson. In 2011, IBM taught it to compete on the game show Jeopardy, where it beat the show's top competitors, not by a bit, but by a mile.

Watson had all of the ingredients of Siri and Snapshot: natural language processing and machine learning to interpret the question (actually, the answer: In addition to everything else it had to do, in keeping with Jeopardy's rules, Watson had to learn to phrase its answers as questions), search through sources, and decide on results using a large computing platform for parallel processing. So vast was the computing platform that the Jeopardy studio was setup at Watson's computing center and not on a traditional network broadcast stage.

By itself, winning Jeopardy was a brilliant PR stunt. Looking to the future, the same capabilities that let Watson find an answer and respond to Alex Trebek in less than a second, and that let it recognize mistakes, learn from them, and adapt its behavior to be an even better contestant, make Watson more of a coal-mine canary than any gracing the previous chapters of this book.

Take IBM's first official attempt to commercialize Watson – medical diagnosis and treatment. Whereas for Jeopardy IBM fed Watson all of Wikipedia (among other information sources), IBM is now feeding it enormous amounts of medical literature. Call the result "Dr. Watson."

Imagine you're a doctor in the very near future, working in a practice that's licensed its own Dr. Watson. You diagnose one of your patients and decide on treatment. Dr. Watson disagrees with your plan of action.

Now what?

Ignore, for the time being, the obvious malpractice aspects of the question. Limit your thinking to your desire to give your patients the best medical care possible. Dr. Watson disagrees with you. Do you override it based on your medical judgment, or do you accept its superior expertise on the grounds that it has digested more medical information than you and your colleagues combined?

Whatever your answer, here's the outcome: Your patient dies.

If you decided to overrule Dr. Watson, you have the guilt that comes from having let your ego interfere with what was obviously the right choice. If, on the other hand, you relied on Dr. Watson's judgment instead of your own, you feel the guilt that comes from taking the easy way out instead of having the courage of your convictions.

And yes, from a malpractice perspective a jury would have to deal with the same conundrum.

In the not so distant future, the medical community will find itself deciding who's in charge, humans or machines.

This by itself isn't all that scary a scenario – there's no reason to expect a Dr. Watson to have ulterior motives, after all. Who/whatever's judgment the medical community decides should prevail, Dr. Watson will be programmed to improve the health of its patients, not to minimize the cost of care, or so we can all hope.

But how about the next generation of algorithmic stock traders? Some company creates a machine to execute high-velocity trading with tools like NLP, machine learning, and autonomous computing. They neglect to instruct it to obey all applicable laws and regulations (we recognize how unlikely this is given the high uniform ethical standards of the field, but go with the assumption, just for this example).

And so the machine executes trade after trade based on its interpretation of events as they unfold. It doesn't just respond at light speed to changes in the marketplace – it uses its ability to manipulate the marketplace, without any human being having any way to shut down the process. And no, nobody can just pull the plug, because so much of the computing takes place in the cloud, where there is no plug to pull.

If marketplace chaos helps this mythical machine turn a profit, we'll have marketplace chaos even before a second trading company installed similar technology.

The next step is to put together the second and third canaries. Imagine some future DeepMind. It isn't just a member of a board of directors. It's the CEO of a corporation. Its installers connect it to a wide variety of news and information sources (the video game display). And they show it where the numbers indicating success reside (bottom-line profit, ROE, EBITDA or what-have-you).

And they turn it loose, forgetting, as in our previous example, to instruct it to obey all applicable laws and regulations.

If that doesn't concern you, imagine the same combination, only now the numbers that indicate success are political polling figures, and instead of game controllers it's wired into Twitter and an automated speechwriting system (precursors of these also exist right now).

The issue isn't the rise of the machines – of computers gaining human-style intelligence and motivations on their own.

To understand why this is unlikely, look at the result of 3 billion years of evolution. No matter what anatomical or behavioral trait you consider, it's evolved on its own, through mutation coupled with natural selection, numerous independent times in different evolutionary lineages.

Except, that is, for human-style consciousness and intelligence. There isn't a shred of evidence to suggest this has happened more than once. That being the case, the Terminator is the least of our concerns.

So ignore the rise of the machines. It isn't going to happen. Which doesn't mean we have nothing to be concerned about as computers become increasingly capable.

The issue isn't defending ourselves against rogue self-motivated machines. It's how we might possibly restrain ourselves from putting machines in charge of everything they do better than we do, which over time might easily turn out to be everything.

Think this is a problem for future business leaders to deal with? Think again. We put computers in charge of human beings quite a long time ago.

Today, we have all kinds of machines that incorporate some form of artificial intelligence that do things for humans. Robot welders. Mail sorters. Virtual service desk agents. And active vehicle driver aids like lane keep assist and collision avoidance.

These types of devices are still controlled by humans. But we also have human beings whose work is paced and tracked by computers, including every customer contact center that employs more than maybe 10 people, and every worker whose assignments come from business process management (BPM) systems. By any reasonable definition, these human beings report to computers.

For them, the machines are already in charge.

Mainframes vs. Personal Computers

What's the difference between a mainframe computer and a PC?

Visualize each one. The mainframe is a big chunk of iron, housed in a carefully engineered data center. A whole crew of specialists takes care of it, like zookeepers making sure the captive giraffe stays healthy.

Figure 10-2. A Mainframe State of Mind

A PC is a small thing that sits on a desk. One person pecks at its keyboard and reviews what's on its screen. The closest thing there is to a crew of specialists looking out for it is the help desk.

But forget all that, because the big difference between mainframes and PCs is conceptual, not physical. Don't ask how big they each are or where they're housed. Instead ask yourself who's in charge. From that perspective there's a universe of difference between the two.

Figure 10-3 depicts a cognitive enterprise built around a mainframe architecture. The machine is in the middle; the role of human beings in a mainframe-centric cognitive enterprise is to feed the machine and keep it happy.

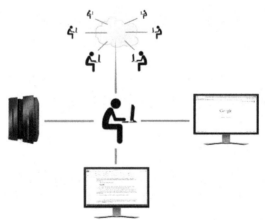

Figure 10-3. Computer-enhanced humanity

The cognition comes from technology. To the extent people

are needed at all, they play a supporting role.

Compare this to Figure 10-2. It's personal computing with emphasis on the personal. In this architecture the human is in the center. Technology serves as a gateway to a universe of capabilities, including personal productivity software, the company's internal systems, various on-line communities, and all the information sources available on the World Wide Web.

Call it computer-enhanced humanity.

The HMRI

Like it or not, the mainframe business architecture will play a major role in the future world of commerce. It will play this role wherever business leaders place a premium on efficiency.

Which is to say, wherever a business continues to play according to the rules of the industrial age.

This isn't going to go away. The rise of the cognitive enterprise isn't going to make industrial ones completely obsolete. There will be a place for mass-produced goods that mostly compete on price for a long, long time to come.

Even many cognitive enterprises are likely to have industrial elements to them.

If there's hope for us humans, it's that cognitive enterprises built around the PC architecture, built, that is, around computer-enhanced human beings, will prove superior to human-fed artificial intelligences.

But first we need a way to keep track. So as a public service we're introducing a new index, to help the world recognize the extent to which humans are still in charge of things. We call this index the human/machine relationship index – the HMRI (Figure 10-4).

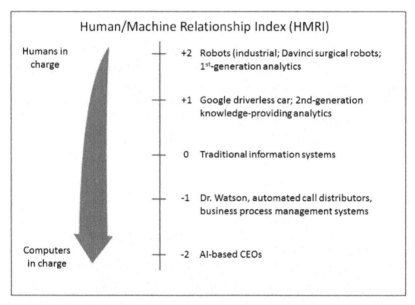

Figure 10-4. the HMRI (human/machine relationship index)

At one end of the HMRI scale are robots – technology that's under the complete control of the human beings who give it instructions. Robots earn a +2 on the HMRI index.

So do the various forms of first-generation analytics systems that provide useful information (in the DIKJW sense of the word introduced in Chapter 5) to human decision-makers.

On the other end of the scale is the AI-based CEO introduced earlier in this chapter. AI-based CEOs receive an HMRI index of -2.

Between these two extremes are such technologies as Google's driverless car, which receives its instructions from human beings but takes care of all the details (HMRI = +1).

Along with driverless cars go the next-generation analytics systems that go beyond information to provide actionable knowledge (again based on the DIKJW framework described in Chapter 5).

Google's driverless car is, as it happens, an excellent example of the non-static nature of HMRI scores. Its predecessor, cruise control, has all the intelligence of a thermostat, which is, by the way, a computer, although a stupendously simple-minded one.

Cruise control gets a +2 on the index. Some future driverless car that detects when an occupant experiences a medical emergency and changes its destination on its own would move the index down into the fractions, still a positive number, but less than +1.

When does the HMRI index equal 0? That score is, interestingly enough, earned by traditional information systems that automate routine tasks like inventory replenishment, but are routinely reviewed and over-ridden by human beings who have access to additional knowledge about the situation.

To finish fleshing out the scale, we'll assign a score of -1 to the ACDs and BPM systems mentioned previously, as human beings program them, but other human beings report to them.

Dr. Watson? It gets a somewhat nervous -1, but for a different reason. It gets a -1 because its role is officially advisory. It's a 1 instead of 0 because Dr. Watson is going to go well beyond offering up knowledge. Dr. Watson attempts to provide judgment.

The HMRI documents movement along the slippery slope that starts with automating the execution of what humans direct to humans executing what a computer directs.

Epilog

Human beings invented the corporation eons ago, as a way to amplify the efforts of individual merchants, in order to achieve increasing scale while limiting the extent to which the investors who own but don't run a business are liable for its actions.

Over time, corporations have increasingly gained the civil rights of human beings, ironically in lockstep inverse proportion to their decreasing humanity. As noted in the introduction to this book, we've reached a point where publicly held corporations operate according to a moral code based on a definition of "good" that's limited to a single variable: Shareholder value.

In more recent times, as businesses have increased their scale by additional orders of magnitude, the industrial model on which they're patterned has prescribed a deliberate dumbing-down. To an ever-greater extent, businesses are replacing human judgment with a drive for efficiency that leads to simplistic reliance on a few ruling metrics.

Which would be just fine if business conditions were stable. But as pointed out early in this little tome, business conditions aren't stable. The numerator of the stay-the-same/change ratio continues to shrink. More and more, the metrics on which business decision makers rely report on how competitive their company is in a marketplace that doesn't exist anymore.

Does this trend toward businesses organized for hyper-standardization and its consequent sprint toward marketplace irrelevancy have to continue?

No.

The premise of this book is a metaphor: That businesses need to recognize the difference between organisms and ecosystems. Most large enterprises are organized as ecosystems. The most successful ones are, and, more importantly, will be *cognitive:* put together to act as organisms – entities that have a societal purpose (missions), clearly understood means through which they turn their missions into profits, and "central nervous systems" built on information technology that itself is cognitive.

Enough with the metaphor. Understand the concept of busi-

202

ness as an organism and a lot of the rest falls into place.

As we hope we have shown in this book, technology can make organism-ness a practical alternative for, if not every enterprise, at least many enterprises. They have the option of becoming cognitive in the sense that the corporation itself makes well-informed decisions, as opposed to individual human beings in the corporation making informed decisions independently. Technology will enable this through a combination of tools that encourage collaboration across organizational boundaries while more broadly sharing important knowledge among the humans, who remain in charge of things, to rely on to make their decisions.

We hope and expect cognitive enterprises will, in addition to being more human, also be more humane. But as we've shown in the last chapter, this outcome is fragile.

We think, or perhaps we just hope, that businesses built on an HMRI +2 foundation will prove more competitive than those that rely on an HMRI of -2.

But for the time being that's just a hope. Our collective challenge will be, to the extent possible, to make this a choice, instead of it just being an outcome we all observe as it happens without our having any say in the matter.

Maybe we should start a business. We'll sell t-shirts emblazoned with Figure 10-3 on the front and "HMRI = +2" on the back. If we do, we'll do our best to make this business cognitive.

We hope you'll follow suit in your own business pursuits.

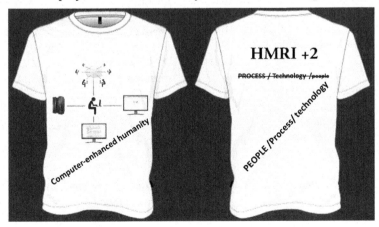

Index

A

Accountability vs Responsibility 168
adaptive case management ... 132, 136
Amazon................................. 108
analytics 80, 85, 98
Apple 58, 107

C

capabilities............................. 121
cognitive business process
    management 132
communities 118
craft....................................... 122
culture 182
curate the data....................... 110
customers............................... 113
Customers, Communities and
    Capabilities............... 102, 127

D

Davenport, Thomas 81
DeepMind.............................. 196
Dell 108
Don't Be Creepy Rule 99

E

Embedded Technology
    Generation (ETG).......... 16, 51
engagement profiling.............. 100
Enterprise Architecture.......... 188

F

fear on performance................. 41

G

Google.................................. 107

H

Human/Machine Relationship
    Index (HMRI) 199

I

IBM Watson........................... 194

J

journey mapping 189
judgment 93

K

kinetic profiles 103
knowledge 91

L

leadership 167

M

mainframe 197
McDonald's............................ 114
media..................................... 115
metrics................... 67, 70, 77, 98
Millennials 15
mission 38

O

OODA loop............................. 95
open source 55

P

People, process, technology 18
Permeability 47
Pervasive Technology Era...... 156

process vs. practice.................128
profiling....................................99
Progressive Insurance.............193
psychographic profiles 101

Q

quality....................................127
quantitative models 69

R

Remote employees 30

S

shadow IT...............................159

socialism...................................43
software agents 142
surveys....................................73

T

teamwork 31
Tesla 55, 57
TOGAF (The Open Group
    Architecture Framework) .. 188

W

wisdom 94

About the Authors

Bob Lewis is well-known in business and information technology circles as a prolific and unconventional commentator on business strategy and organization, information technology organizations and what makes them tick, how businesses should use and think about technology, and, most important, leadership and business change.

Before becoming a consultant and industry commentator he did real work in real corporations. Since then his consulting has taken him into dozens of businesses of all sizes, industries and styles, where he has provided advice and guidance on issues ranging from incremental improvements to organizational effectiveness to planning and organizing all-encompassing enterprise transformations.

He's the author of eleven books and more than 1,500 columns on these and related subjects. About past books readers have said:

- Bob Lewis is one of the clearest, and clearest-thinking, writers on management and leadership I know. His insights and advice are spot-on, very well expressed and lightened with just the right amount of humor.
- I find Mr. Lewis's practical wisdom really hits the spot.
- This book was a god send. It's written as a guide book full of practical tips without sounding the least bit like a consultant's brainchild.
- This book is a well-rounded package of excellent, up-to-date, real world advice.
- This book is like a breath of fresh air blowing away stale hyperbole.
- This should be required reading for all Boards of Directors and all Government leaders (MPs, Congressmen, Senators etc.) plus all of us in middle (and junior) management. Oh and it is still a slim book which is almost impossible to put down! Amazing for a really great 'management text'!

Currently, Mr. Lewis is a senior principal consultant with Dell Services Digital Business Consulting group, where he heads its next-generation IT community of practice.

Scott Lee is a technologist, entrepreneur and change agent. As a technologist, he frequently teaches organizations of all sizes how to apply technology to differentiate from their competition. His expertise in digital technology is evident in dozens of venues such as college campuses, healthcare facilities, sports stadiums, online banks and vehicle telematics.

As an entrepreneur, he developed a utility computing model within a large telecommunications data center that is now a standard for the Telco's private cloud operations. As a change agent, he has helped organizations move from rigid deployment models to agile methods that enable continuous integration and deployment.

When he's not challenging business leaders to embrace change, he can be found fidgeting with new technology or observing its use within our culture.

Mr. Lee is the professional services practice lead for enterprise architecture within Dell Services Digital Business Consulting group, where he advises on the development of advanced business consulting services.

Acknowledgements

First and foremost, before we thank anyone else, we have to thank all the people who did so much to develop many of the concepts you'll find in this book. We have no idea who they are, but we're well aware that the knowledge we've gained over the years about what does and doesn't work came from somewhere. Enough of it came out of our pointy little heads that we can take credit for there being some originality in these pages.

But we're pretty sure that most of what we know (or think we know) came from conversations we've had, presentations we've listened to, and material we've read over the years.

So if you read something here and think to yourself, "Those *%&#$ so-called experts took my idea and are claiming credit for it!" rest assured of two things.

One is that we're declaring, here and now, that if someone else reads your idea and likes it, our failing is in not remembering that you were the source.

The other is that we're in the same boat. One of us (Bob Lewis) has, in fact, written more than 1,500 columns and 12 books (including this one) over a span of 20 years and frequently sees ideas he's published offered as original thinking by others. Fair's fair, and symmetry is a hallmark of fairness. So get over it.

People we know deserve credit for some of what's here. In no particular order:

Okay, these two are in particular order: Our wives, Sharon Link and Belinda Lee not only showed remarkable patience as we took what turned out to be quite a lot of time to write this puppy, they both actively encouraged us to take this on. This was far above and beyond the call of duty. Thank you!

Anita Cassidy, author of the popular *A Practical Guide to Information Systems Planning* and several other books of great value provided valuable enhancements to our developing manuscript in what she laughingly calls her spare time, as she has for previous books authored by the Bob Lewis half of this book's partnership.

The same goes for Dave Kaiser. We'd write more, but it

would just be saying the same things in different words. Although Dave was Bob's co-author in their worst-selling novel, *The Moral Hazard of Lime Daiquiris*. Calling that a book of great value might be a bit of a stretch.

Tom Vogel read the entire manuscript. Twice – once in its *societal enterprise* form and again after it had become *Cognition*. We're grateful, not only for his stamina, but also for his encouragement and suggestions.

We thank Peter Fingar, our publisher and author of 23+ business and technology books including the most recent, *Cognitive Computing*. The moment he discovered, through casual mention, that we were writing this tome, he asked "Why don't I publish it?" We couldn't think of a good reason (from our perspective) why he shouldn't. And so he is our publisher.

John DuBois, who leads Dell Services' Digital Business Consulting organization, of which both authors are a part, reviewed the societal-enterprise version of the manuscript and was instrumental in helping us see the need to redirect and sharpen our focus. He did so, we hasten to add, on his own time, not Dell time.

We're also grateful to Jim Stikeleather, who through one of those strange coincidences turned out to be Peter Fingar's collaborator and coauthor of *Next Generation Business* and the most recent, *Business Innovation in the Cloud*. Jim and Peter both provided comments so knowledgeable and insightful we're grateful they didn't think to attack this topic first.

Jim, by the way, is another Dell guy who, we hasten to add, did his reviewing on personal, not Dell, time.

Likewise the time we spent writing it. While we're grateful to John and, by extension, Dell, for encouraging us to pursue this project, this is in no way a manuscript sanctioned or in any way influenced by Dell. Which means it's disclaimer time:

Disclaimer: The thoughts, ideas, concepts, prescriptions, proscriptions, formulas, hypotheses, frameworks, and, for that matter, half-witted notions we'll regret having published someday, are our own. It is in no way to be considered a Dell or Dell-endorsed product.

Companion Books from Meghan-Kiffer Press

Cognitive Computing
A Brief Guide for Game Changers

Business Architecture
The Art and Practice of Business Transformation

Dot Cloud
The 21st Century business Platform Built on Cloud Computing

Business Innovation in the Cloud
Strategies for Executing on Innovation with Cloud Computing

Value Networks
And the True Nature of Collaboration

Smart Process Apps
The Next Breakout Business Advantage

Human Interactions
The Heart and Soul of Business Process Management

Enterprise Cloud Computing
A Strategy Guide for Business and Technology Leaders

Extreme Competition
Innovation and the Great 21st Century Business Reformation

Business Process Management
The Third Wave

Business Process Management
The Next Wave

Mastering the Unpredictable
How Adaptive Case Management Will Revolutionize
the Way That Knowledge Workers Get Things Done

See more at...

www.mkpress.com

Innovation at the Intersection of Business and Technology